T0103311

The Dark Lady

Pandora

The Dark Lady

Pandora

Two plays by Jessica B. Hill

SCIROCCO DRAMA

The Dark Lady
Pandora
first published 2024 by Scirocco Drama
An imprint of J. Gordon Shillingford Publishing Inc.
© 2024 Jessica B. Hill

Excerpt on Page 116 from *Reality Is Not What It Seems: The Journey to Quantum Gravity* by Carlo Rovelli, copyright © 2014 by Rafaello Cortina Editore SpA, translation copyright © 2016 by Simon Carnell and Erica Segre. Used by permission of Riverhead, an imprint of Penguin Publishing Group, a division of Penguin Random House LLC. All rights reserved.

Scirocco Drama Editor: Glenda MacFarlane
Cover design by Doowah Design
Author photo by Ted Belton
The Dark Lady production photos by Leif Norman
Pandora production photos by Joey Senft.

Printed and bound in Canada on 100% post-consumer recycled paper.

Production inquiries to:
Ian Arnold, Catalyst TCM
PO Box 98074
RPO Queen and Carlaw
Toronto ON   M4M 3L9
ian@catalysttcm.com
1.416.568.8673

Library and Archives Canada Cataloguing in Publication

Title: The dark lady ; Pandora / two plays by Jessica B. Hill.
Other titles: Dark lady (Compilation) | Pandora
Names: Hill, Jessica B., author. | Container of (expression): Hill, Jessica B. Dark lady. | Container of (expression): Hill, Jessica B. Pandora.
Identifiers: Canadiana 20240355970 | ISBN 9781990738357 (softcover)
Subjects: LCGFT: Drama.
Classification: LCC PS8615.I468 D37 2024 | DDC C812/.6—dc23

We acknowledge the financial support of the Canada Council for the Arts, the Government of Canada, the Manitoba Arts Council, and the Manitoba Government for our publishing program.

J. Gordon Shillingford Publishing
P.O. Box 86, RPO Corydon Avenue, Winnipeg, MB Canada R3M 3S3

*To my father for the storytelling, my mother for the poetry,
Jeremy for the grit, and Rodrigo for the dream*

Jessica B. Hill

Jessica is a bilingual actor, playwright and teacher originally from Montreal. *Pandora* and *The Dark Lady* marked her playwriting debut in 2023 with both having their world premiere productions within months of each other in Winnipeg and Saskatoon. Calgary welcomed a subsequent production of *The Dark Lady* within the same year.

Jessica has spent eight seasons acting at the Stratford Festival, starring as Viola in *Twelfth Night*, Helena in *All's Well that Ends Well* and Lady Anne in *Richard III*. She has performed in both English and French on stage, on screen, in voicework and in games.

A graduate of Stratford Festival's Birmingham Conservatory, McGill University and Dawson College, she is also a visiting instructor at the National Theatre School of Canada, teaching Chekhov and Shakespeare.

Playwright's Notes

Live theatre creates a bridge between ourselves and the other.

It helps us see each other *in* each other.

That's what drives me as a performer and as a writer: the act of fostering a meaningful connection, a tether of truth, between myself and someone else. It's an act of love, of radical hope: it's a leap of faith. We're all wrestling with the great unknown, the need for meaning, the answer to the question "Where do I belong? Why am I here and what am I going to do about it?" Our individual existences are solitary experiences, and yet, that's the exact fact that ties us all together across time. I still remember laughing at ancient Viking runes, etched on the wall of an even-more-ancient Neolithic cave, that simply translated to "Haermund Hardaxe was here."[1]

It's a marvel how similar we are.

We all want to leave our mark. We are all trying to understand and make meaning of our place in the world. What of us lives on, whose story gets told, what kind of love or art can never be destroyed? What is the legacy we are leaving? I think both plays address this in different ways.

The Dark Lady allowed me to explore these questions from a marginalized perspective. Researchers have now revealed Shakespeare's London to be a much more multicultural place than we had all been led to believe. His beloved plays began to open themselves to me in a new way and allowed me to rediscover them through my own lens. *The Dark Lady* also offered me an intimate window into these two historical

---

[1] *Viking graffiti on Maeshowe, a Neolithic cairn in Orkney, reads "Haermund Hardaxe carved these runes"*

figures' hearts, minds, and shared humanity. The play may be fiction, but Emilia Bassano-Lanier's life truly does seem to encompass the breadth of Shakespeare's work. The compounding historical coincidences in timelines, verse lines, friends in common, are astonishing…and delicious. It felt like uncovering a 400-year-old mystery. As if Time were untangling a secret knot. As if I was stumbling on ancient etchings waiting to be discovered, that simply said "I was here."

Pandora fed a fascination I've always had about the similarities between art and science. They both help us make sense of the world and give us drastically different yet complementary lenses on what we call reality. An act of theatre needs an audience to exist, and it's different every time you see it. Until then, it's just the possibility of a performance in an empty space. Funnily, that statement can also apply to quantum mechanics, a field of science so strange it skirts with philosophy.

As a child, I remember I fully expected life to come with a user manual. I assumed someone would hand it over when I turned eighteen, maybe there'd be an orientation video. Cue my consternation as I began to realize everyone was out there improvising everything. The idea for *Pandora* arose from that memory.

A character on a quest to clear her name. To make sense of how the world works. To weave a story from uncertainty.

We are creatures of story. In times of darkness, we reach for myth.

Creating these plays was a beautifully collaborative effort, I feel deep gratitude for everyone involved. A special thanks to Kate Hennig and Bob White, for their deft dramaturgy, mentorship, love and belief. To jaymez, our production designer on *Pandora*, who imbued the piece with brilliant virtuosity to create intricate, awe-inspiring cosmic magic. And a special, heartfelt thanks to Rodrigo Beilfuss for being my beacon and touchstone through both these plays' creation. Thank you for encouraging me to write.

In writing both pieces, I've spent time thinking about all the people who come into our lives and expand who we are: caring words, actions, teachings, books, guidance that stays with us forever. In some quiet way, we are dreamed into being through our connections. All of us, sublime mosaics of one another.

Is that poetry, or is it quantum entanglement?

…who knows?

All I know is that this is your story too.

Jessica

Foreword

When theatres shut down in the spring of 2020, my friend and often collaborator Jessica was about to open a killer season at Stratford; she was set to play leading roles in two big Shakespearean productions — a dream season, as I remember her telling me. And then everything came crashing down.

There were plenty of jokes going around then, via cheeky online memes, about Shakespeare writing epic poems and King Lear during his plague and lockdown days, but no one really took those unique achievements seriously as a possibility that someone else could do the same now. And then Jessica did it.

She became a playwright-actress, and I was lucky enough to be the friend, dramaturge and director that she shared her thoughts, desires and new plays with. Within the last three years of the plague, Jessica has written three plays and has so far scheduled four professional productions of her works (two of them are now published, and you hold them in your hands); with shows in Alberta, Ontario, Saskatchewan and Winnipeg all taking place between 2022 and 2023. And there are more readings, productions and playwrighting commissions scheduled for 2024. My friend is unstoppable. We are so lucky to be alive now in the Age of Jess!

Somehow, I don't feel at all surprised by Jessica's meteoric rise since the plague hit in 2020. In June of that year, my daughter was born, and I remember very vividly spending sleepless nights lying on the floor of my baby's bedroom as she struggled to fall asleep; and one night playing in my ears a recording of Jessica reading the very first draft of *The Dark Lady*…and quite quickly I thought to myself, There it is, there's a full play in the making there, Jessica has struck gold!

And the rest is history. You're holding the latest version of that story in your hands right now. That important tale about the complex nature of creation, and (alleged) complicated relationship between two titanic historical figures, has finally been written after four centuries of speculation. Somewhere, up in the clouds, within the borders of the undiscovered country, Shakespeare is smiling and blushing.

In early 2023, before we finally collaborated on the full production of *The Dark Lady* in the spring, we delivered the world-premiere of *Pandora* in a very dark and cold Winnipeg winter. A solo piece about Greek mythology, quantum mechanics, the plague, and molecular and metaphysical interconnectedness somehow became a beacon of hope and joy during a very sombre season. Winnipeg audiences fell in love with Jessica then.

You see, Jessica has this ability to communicate incredibly complex ideas and contradictory emotions in a way that is not only accessible (in the friendliest meaning of the word), but utterly pleasurable. As an artist, she operates from a place of absolute kindness and warmth. She is driven by curiosity and passion. Her wish is to connect with YOU in a way that truly astonishes you into feeling alive. It is such a beautiful gift that she has and openly chooses to share with us.

Whether Jessica is writing about Shakespeare or Greek demi-gods, the impulse is the same and the generosity is boundless: she chooses hope.

When the world went dark and the very form of theatre dissolved, she wrestled with her demons like we all did, and then she chose to put pen to paper—first to save herself, and then sharing the findings to save us.

We are so lucky. I am so lucky to know her as a dear friend. I can't wait to see what else she discovers to light up our lives with.

I hope you enjoy reading her words with great pleasure and wonder.

Muito amor, xo

Rodrigo Beilfuss

September 2023

Rodrigo Beilfuss is the artistic director of Shakespeare in the Ruins (SIR), and was the director of the premiere productions of Pandora *and* The Dark Lady.

The Dark Lady

"I don't know why, but I always feel something Italian, something Jewish about Shakespeare, and perhaps Englishmen admire him because of that, because it's so unlike them."

—Jorge Luis Borges

Acknowledgements

Rodrigo Beilfuss, Kate Hennig, Fiona Mongillo, Skye Brandon, Yvette Nolan, Kayvon Khoshkam, Sarah Malabar, Melanie Rogowski, Brian Drader, Antoni Cimolino, Dave Auster, Keith Barker, Bob White, Michael Hart, Rylan Wilkie, Eric Blais, George Bajer-Koulack, Emma Welham, Daina Leitold, Brenda McLean, Paige Lewis, Evan King, Cari Simpson, TL Kosinski, Claire Sparling, Myren Mallory Philpot, Siobhan O'Malley, Ijeoma Emesowum, Tim Bratton, Mara Teare, Terry Gallagher, Leif Norman, Scott Wentworth and Marion Adler, Seana McKenna and Miles Potter, Lucy Peacock, Bronwyn Steinberg, Luigi Riscaldino, Natascha Girgis, Professor Paul Yachnin, Amanda Kellock and the wonderful group she assembled for our weekly Shakespeare video conversations that buoyed me through the 2020 pandemic: Quincy Armorer, Michelle Boulet, Paul Budra, James MacDonald, Randall Martin, Alison Matthews, Andre Hendges, Nicholas Leno, Noah Millman, Gretchen Minton, Ahmed Moneka, Lawrence Flores Pereira, Amelia Sargisson, Jeremy Smith and Antoine Yared.

Mom, Dad and Jeremy for their love and belief.

I cherish the memory of Ian Watson and Martha Henry who fostered, galvanized and deepened my love of Shakespeare.

Thank you.

Production History

The first draft of *The Dark Lady* was originally commissioned by Here for Now Theatre for a public reading in August 2020.

It subsequently underwent a workshop and public staged reading with The Stratford Festival as part of their Meighen Forum in August of 2021 and was the unofficial first public event at the new Tom Patterson Theatre. The workshop and reading were directed by Rodrigo Beilfuss with dramaturgy by Kate Hennig and Bob White and stage management by Michael Hart. The cast was Jessica B. Hill and Rylan Wilkie.

The Dark Lady was first produced as a co-production between Shakespeare in the Ruins (SIR) and Shakespeare on the Saskatchewan. It opened in Winnipeg on June 15th, 2023 and transferred to Saskatoon on July 6th, 2023. The play was commissioned and developed through SIR's Brave New Works program with support from the Manitoba Association of Playwrights (MAP) and Shakespeare on the Saskatchewan through a series of workshops and public readings. The premiere cast and creative team was as follows:

Emilia Bassano	Jessica B. Hill
William Shakespeare	Eric Blais
Live Musician	George Bajer-Koulack
Director	Rodrigo Beilfuss
Assistant Director	Emma Welham
Music Director	George Bajer-Koulack
Costume Designer	Brenda McLean
Props and Set Designer	Daina Leitold
Stage Manager	Paige Lewis
Stage Manager (Saskatoon)	Aaron Shingoose

The Dark Lady received a second production three months later in Calgary, a co-production between Lunchbox Theatre and The Shakespeare Company. It opened at the Vertigo Theatre on October 12th, 2023, with the following cast and creative team.

Emilia Bassano .... Natascha Grigis

William Shakespeare .... Luigi Riscaldino

Director .... Bronwyn Steinberg

Stage Manager .... Carissa Sams

Set Designer .... Madeline Blondal

Lighting Designer .... Lisa Floyd

Sound Designer .... Alixandra Cowman

Costume Designer .... Rebecca Toon

"Now you are me and I am you." Emilia (Jessica B. Hill) and Shakespeare (Eric Blais) trade clothing. Photography: Leif Norman.

"As if heaven opens and gives them both a glimpse at the everlasting." Emilia (Jessica B. Hill) shares a story with Shakespeare (Eric Blais). Photography: Leif Norman.

"The twangling of the strings would rock me to sleep." Musician and musical director (George Bajer-Koulack) underscores the performance. Photography: Leif Norman.

"The first female professional poet on English soil." Emilia (Jessica B. Hill) publishes her poetry. Photography: Leif Norman.

Production Notes

On casting:

Emilia must visually convey the image of someone from a diaspora that has been othered, racialized and marginalized. Someone whose cultural and racial history and identity have not been centre stage historically.

Ideally, she should have dark skin, dark hair and dark eyes.

It's possible the historical Emilia Bassano had Sephardic, Italian, African, Arabic and/or Spanish lineage. She had a mixed-race identity. Elizabethans referred to her musician cousins as Black men.

Shakespeare must be able to visually convey a sense of cultural, racial, ethnic privilege in his society. Though he comes from a small town and has been less educated than he would have liked, he has benefitted from the privilege of his sex, race and culture.

On music and transitions:

Music is central to Emilia's family line and narrative. The play benefits from a special attention given to music and its capacity to transport, create space and distend time. The musical titles are starting-off points and can be used for inspiration.

The premiere production featured a live guitarist onstage scoring the entire play. The live music imbued the world of the play with lyricism, immediacy and intimacy.

Transitions can help to enhance the passage of time. For example, a shawl can become a baby, bedsheets can become togas, and a willow tree can feature as the couple's mailbox.

Characters

Emilia Bassano

William Shakespeare

The characters will age thirty years within the scope of the play.

Setting

Here. Now. But also there, then.

Actors should use their normal voices and accents. It is more important that the characters feel relatable than feel period.

ACT I

Leitmotif

"A recurring theme associated with a particular person"

> *A swell of music. A courtly dance. EMILIA and SHAKESPEARE have been eyeing each other from across the room. They approach one another.*

EMILIA: You were watching me play the piano all night.

SHAKESPEARE: Didn't I dance with you at Hampton once?

EMILIA: No. I don't think so.

SHAKESPEARE: I'm sure we did.

EMILIA: Then why would you bother asking the question?

SHAKESPEARE: I'd remember that hair and those entrancing eyes anywhere.

EMILIA: *(Savouring the word.)* "Entrancing," nice.

SHAKESPEARE: You'd be impossible to forget.

EMILIA: And yet, it seems like you have.

SHAKESPEARE: Not in the least.

> *Beat.*

EMILIA: You know, you were ogling me then, too.

SHAKESPEARE: *(Savouring the word.)* "Ogling"? Nice. I thought I was being discreet.

EMILIA: You weren't.

SHAKESPEARE: *(Aha!)* So then you admit it: we met.

EMILIA: Not only did we meet but you wrote me an entire sonnet, on the spot.

SHAKESPEARE: I do that sometimes.

                 It must have come to me as I watched you play.

EMILIA: It's a great party trick.
                 Must work like a charm with most ladies.

SHAKESPEARE: Most.
                 Though...I never did catch your name.

EMILIA: You never bothered to ask.

                 Beat.

SHAKESPEARE: I distinctly remember you complimenting me on my performance.

EMILIA: I distinctly remember you complimenting me on mine.

SHAKESPEARE: Well, your music is exquisite.

EMILIA: *"Exquisite"* ...huh.
                 That's the word you used last time.

                 Beat.

SHAKESPEARE: And what about me?

EMILIA: What about you?

SHAKESPEARE: Did you like the play tonight?

EMILIA: *...The Two Gentlemen of Verona?*

SHAKESPEARE: I wrote it.

EMILIA: You wrote it?

SHAKESPEARE: Yup.

EMILIA: Wow.

SHAKESPEARE: *(Cocky.)* I know.

EMILIA: So *you're* William Shakespeare!

SHAKESPEARE: My name's been getting around, I see!

EMILIA: I've seen your plays.

SHAKESPEARE: All three?

EMILIA: A lot of "History of England" hype.

SHAKESPEARE: Crowd-pleasing Classics.

EMILIA: But this *new* one, it's a very different genre for you.

SHAKESPEARE: Expanding the repertoire.

EMILIA: And you set it in Italy!

SHAKESPEARE: *(Corrects her with flair.) Italia:* "The land of romance and mystique, where anything can happen!"

EMILIA: Have you been?

SHAKESPEARE: Nope.
                But people love that stuff, it's a huge draw!

                Our company's looking for a new sponsor, gotta pull out all the stops.

                    Beat.

EMILIA: Mr. Shakespeare—

SHAKESPEARE: You can call me Will.

EMILIA: I've been wanting to meet you, Will.

SHAKESPEARE: Well, turns out you have, twice.

EMILIA: We need to talk about that ending.

SHAKESPEARE: What about it?

EMILIA: You're extremely talented.

SHAKESPEARE: Thank you.

EMILIA: But you're shit at writing women.

SHAKESPEARE: Alright, lady, take it easy.

EMILIA: They start off great! But you always seem to silence them at the exact moment they should be at their loudest. It's infuriating.

SHAKESPEARE: I don't recall ever asking you for notes.

EMILIA: Do you really see it as a happy ending?

SHAKESPEARE: It is a comedy, isn't it?

EMILIA: Your first comedy.

SHAKESPEARE: Yes.

EMILIA: It shows.

SHAKESPEARE: Gotta say, you were much more pleasant from afar.

EMILIA: Trust me, a woman would have said something.

SHAKESPEARE: What is this? You're speaking for all womankind now?

EMILIA: If it had been me you wouldn't have heard the end of it.

SHAKESPEARE: Yeah, so I'm starting to gather.

Good thing you're not in my play, you sound like a lot to handle.

EMILIA: I'm just interested in a more complex female character.
A woman with some agency.

SHAKESPEARE: Where does a musician get off thinking they can tell me how to write?

EMILIA: Oh, I write too.

SHAKESPEARE: You do?

EMILIA: I wrote you a little sonnet, on the spot.
It came to me while I watched your play.

SHAKESPEARE: You write *sonnets*?

She hands him a folded paper.

He reads.

SHAKESPEARE: Who *are* you?

EMILIA: Emilia Bassano.

SHAKESPEARE: Emilia Bassano.
(Putting two and two together.) Bassano...Like those court musicians?

EMILIA: Yup.

SHAKESPEARE: Those Venetians who play for the Queen.

EMILIA: Yup. All my uncles.

SHAKESPEARE: I work with those guys all the time! John—

EMILIA: *(Correcting him.)* Giovanni

SHAKESPEARE: Jasper

EMILIA: Jacomo

SHAKESPEARE: Alvise

EMILIA : Alvixe

SHAKESPEARE: And Antonio.

EMILIA: And Antonio.

SHAKESPEARE: He's good people, Antonio.

EMILIA: He really is.

Beat.

SHAKESPEARE: Big family.

EMILIA: *Italians.*

Beat.

SHAKESPEARE: ...but are you though?

EMILIA: What?

SHAKESPEARE: You hear rumours, you know?

EMILIA: Oh, do you?

Beat.

SHAKESPEARE: You really don't *look* Italian.

EMILIA: Well, if you've never been, how would you know?

SHAKESPEARE: ...Touché.

Beat.

SHAKESPEARE: Is it true you're secretly Jewish?

EMILIA: Is it true you're a social-climbing, arrogant prick?

SHAKESPEARE: Yowch!

EMILIA: I know, rumours. Dangerous.

                   Beat. A levelling out and a more intimate opening as they show their cards.

SHAKESPEARE: Aren't you The Lord Chamberlain's mistress?

EMILIA: I call him Henry.
                   Aren't you married with kids up in the country somewhere?

SHAKESPEARE: Stratford.

EMILIA: How many?

SHAKESPEARE: Three: Judith, Susanna and Hamnet.

EMILIA: Wow.

                   Stalemate.

                   Pause.

EMILIA: Tell you what.
                   The Lord Chamberlain is interested in sponsoring a new theatre company.
                   …And I wanted William Shakespeare to be the writer.
                   I could put a word in.

SHAKESPEARE: Y—you would? I thought you just said you hated my writing.

EMILIA: I hated your ending. Your writing is… *exquisite.*

SHAKESPEARE: *(Oh.)* Oh.

EMILIA: But I need you to do something for me too.

SHAKESPEARE: What can I do for you?

EMILIA: Write me a woman who fights for what she wants.

Interlude

"Music between Music"

> *Music plays. Fantasia 5, number 3 by Jeronimo Bassano or music inspired by this piece.*
>
> *In all her soliloquies, Emilia is speaking to Shakespeare outside of linear time.*
> *As if we were catching scattered moments through their entire relationship.*
> *Even if spoken to the audience, his presence (or later on, absence) should be felt in them all.*

EMILIA: What does it really mean to belong?

I was born here.
But my father settled in Italy,
my grandfather wandered West-Africa,
my great-grandfather fled from Spain.

We're from… everywhere.

Our family had to change names, often.
Had to move. Had to learn to adapt, fast.
Our story runs along the margins of history.
Off the record.
So, where do I come from?

> *It dawns on her as she takes in the music.*

…Music.
We were music well before we were even Bassanos.

> *She listens.*

This is my grandfather's composition.
Jeronimo Bassano.

One day, I was rummaging through a bunch of his old books that my father had brought with him from Venice.

Oh, you should know this about me:
I love old books, the bigger, the older, the better.
They've *endured*…you know?
They're real. Lasting. Tactile.
And… they smell amazing!
They smell like what I imagine knowledge should smell like.

Brittle, yellowed paper.
Sour, leathery musk.
And a hint of sea salt telling me how far they've travelled.

But that day, amongst the books…

She pulls out a giant tome.

I found a Bible.
My grandfather's Bible.
From when the Spanish forced him to convert.

What initially caught my eye was the repetition of the name Bassano on the first few pages. Over and over.
As he practised his new signature.

A kind of imprint of himself.
A need to make a mark.

And then, I read his scribbles in the margins.
My musician grandfather had translated the New Testament into Hebrew!
An act of rebellion? Of self-reclamation?

And, at the very back of the book he wrote in four different languages:

"Sufferance is the badge of all our tribe."

I want to imagine four, five hundred years from now, there'll be a Bassano, or whatever else we'll go by then, playing this same song.

Our story may be written in sand, but some things can't ever be lost.

Some things simply are, and have always been...

They just need time to reemerge from the dark.

Contrapuntal Fugue

"Two melodic voices, independent but related harmonically"

> *Post-theatrical performance. Shakespeare is packing up scattered props and costumes... a broken lute perhaps. EMILIA approaches.*

SHAKESPEARE: Emilia Bassano.

EMILIA: William Shakespeare.

SHAKESPEARE: Were you there tonight?

EMILIA: Oh, I was.

SHAKESPEARE: Any notes?

EMILIA: She fights, all right.

SHAKESPEARE: She's fire.

EMILIA: And instead of silencing her, you gave her the largest speech of the play.

SHAKESPEARE: I don't think a woman like that would ever be quiet.

EMILIA: The largest speech…praising how great the man is.

SHAKESPEARE: *(Grins.)*…too cheeky?

EMILIA: *The Taming of the Shrew?*

SHAKESPEARE: Too cheeky.

EMILIA: I think you'd find me impossible to tame.

SHAKESPEARE: Is that a challenge?

EMILIA: It's a warning.

SHAKESPEARE: I haven't been known to heed warnings…

EMILIA: So I've heard. *(Then, suspicious.)* My father's name was Baptista.

SHAKESPEARE: …I may have chatted with a Bassano or two.

                  Antonio let a few things slip.

EMILIA: Uh huh.

                  Beat. They both see Henry Carey across the room and SHAKESPEARE notices EMILIA stiffen.

SHAKESPEARE: Tell me, what's the deal with you and the Lord Chamberlain…?

EMILIA: Henry?

SHAKESPEARE: He's a bit old for you, no?

EMILIA: He's 70.

SHAKESPEARE: So what's the arrangement… does he pay you well or—?

EMILIA: Oh my God. You are terrible at this.

SHAKESPEARE: No, I'm just… I want to know more about you.

EMILIA: I was presented with a hard choice to make and I made it.

SHAKESPEARE: A choice between?

EMILIA: The bonds of marriage and a kind of freedom.

SHAKESPEARE: And, *is* it freedom?

EMILIA: Well…I wouldn't be able to write poetry or play music if I'd been forced to marry the glover down the street.

SHAKESPEARE: Hey. My father was a glover.

EMILIA: Oh shit, sorry. No offence.

SHAKESPEARE: None taken.
                  I didn't want to be a glover either.

EMILIA: …is that why you ran away?

SHAKESPEARE: I didn't… run. I visit when I can.

EMILIA: Oh boy. Okay.
                  So what's the deal with you?

SHAKESPEARE: There's a part of me that can't exist over there…
                  I found a compromise.

EMILIA: Between?

SHAKESPEARE: …The bonds of marriage and a kind of freedom.

EMILIA: That's a hell of a sacrifice.

SHAKESPEARE: I could say the same to you.

EMILIA: It is not ideal.

SHAKESPEARE: So I need to make it worth it.

EMILIA: Exactly!

                   A beat of recognition.

                   Then.

EMILIA: Do they live happily ever after?

SHAKESPEARE: Who? Petruchio and Kate?

EMILIA: Yeah.

SHAKESPEARE: I'd say probably happier than most.

EMILIA: Really?? Why is that?

SHAKESPEARE: They found their dynamic.
                   In the end, men just want to be admired and
                   women want to be cherished, no?

EMILIA: …Huh.

SHAKESPEARE: What?
                   Where's the snappy comeback?

EMILIA: You're smarter than you look.

SHAKESPEARE: Is that a compliment?

EMILIA: Hold on…

                   She pulls out an old leather-bound book.

SHAKESPEARE: What's this?

EMILIA: Reading material.
                   It's from my family's library.
                   Boccaccio.

SHAKESPEARE: I've heard of him.

EMILIA: Well, now you can *read* him.
                   Just, take care of it, okay?

> *SHAKESPEARE instinctively takes a long whiff, EMILIA notices, delighted.*

SHAKESPEARE: …It smells amazing.

EMILIA: Maybe you'll find some… *inspiration.*

SHAKESPEARE: *(Chuckles.)* Nice.
Uh…hold on… this entire thing's in Italian!

EMILIA: Yeah. I translated in the margins.

SHAKESPEARE: The whole book?

EMILIA: The whole book.
Read. Then tell me what you think.

Interlude 2

"Music between Music"

> *Music, a repeat of Jeronimo Bassano's composition. Perhaps a variation from it. EMILIA recognizes it.*

EMILIA: When I was little, my father would sandwich me between the lute and his chest, and play this piece!
The twangling of the strings rocking me to sleep.

Where do the notes go after we can't hear them?
They seem to reverberate in the air fainter and fainter until they disappear…

But what if they don't? What if instead, they float up, up, beyond the clouds and then hang there like stars, suspended in the firmament.

Because sometimes a harmony can be so sweet, it's as if those clouds part, and all the sounds and airs, every melody that has ever been played, can faintly be heard again.

She outstretches her arms to the sky.

As if Heaven opens… and cascades rivers of music down upon my head.
So sweet a strain, I cry to hear again.
…

I like watching you watching me play… your face softens and I can see the little boy you once were.

Chromatic Modulation

"A progression involving chromatic inflection between keys that are not closely related"

> *A play at Court is about to begin, EMILIA is sitting in the audience, watching the musicians setting up. SHAKESPEARE sidles towards her.*

SHAKESPEARE: Miss Bassano.

EMILIA: Mister Shakespeare.

SHAKESPEARE: Is this seat taken?

EMILIA: Sit at your own risk.

SHAKESPEARE: A risk I'd gladly take.

EMILIA: You're not in your play tonight?

SHAKESPEARE: I thought I'd sit this one out and watch with you instead.

There are your uncles. *(Waves.)*

EMILIA: There are my uncles. *(Waves.)*

   Beat.

SHAKESPEARE: I heard about your cousin.

   She bristles but stays silent.

SHAKESPEARE: How is he?

EMILIA: Ill.

SHAKESPEARE: And you?

EMILIA: Ill too.

SHAKESPEARE: They arrested him?

   She nods.

SHAKESPEARE: On what grounds?

EMILIA: For looking "suspicious." He's in the Tower.

SHAKESPEARE: God. Why did he start the fight?

EMILIA: He didn't.

SHAKESPEARE: Everyone's saying he did. And with a nobleman, too.

EMILIA: Some nobleman. That guy had been taunting him for weeks. He kept calling him "A Thing of Darkness" or "Black Devil."

SHAKESPEARE: Really?

EMILIA: Finally, he answered, "If there be devils, I wish I was one so I could torture you in hell." And he lunged.
   But you tell me who started it.

SHAKESPEARE: That's blasphemous. They're going to think he's a monster.

EMILIA: No, that's the point, Will. They already do.

SHAKESPEARE: But they could lock him up forever.
                It was too rash...he should have kept a low
                profile.

EMILIA: So he should just smile at the guy spitting in
                his face?

SHAKESPEARE: No, of course not.

                But won't hate just breed hate?

EMILIA: Won't cruelty just teach cruelty?

                Beat.

SHAKESPEARE: Has this happened to him often?

EMILIA: It's his third arrest this month.

SHAKESPEARE: For looking different.

EMILIA: For *seeming* different.

                *Beat. She's not sure how to get through to
                him.*

EMILIA: Will.

                Have I told you I speak six languages?

SHAKESPEARE: No.

EMILIA: I speak six languages.

SHAKESPEARE: That's—

EMILIA: I play four instruments.

SHAKESPEARE: Okay.

EMILIA: That book I lent you, there's more where that
                came from.

                I have an extensive library.

SHAKESPEARE: Extensive?

EMILIA: Extensive.

SHAKESPEARE: Well that's...great?

EMILIA: *(She can't look at him as she tries to explain.)* I'm trying to tell you something.

I was schooled by nobility. I got impossibly lucky.

A Countess took a shine to me and taught me history, philosophy, literature, Latin, Greek...

I'm as "learnèd" as they come... but I have nowhere to put it.

That's why I write.

Because they can't hear what I have to say beyond what they've been told to see.

Beat.

SHAKESPEARE: *(Overcome.)* Emilia.

That's.... ever since I met you....I've...

I don't want my work to just be frivolous, entertaining fluff.

I want to make people question how things are.

EMILIA: I want to change how they are.

SHAKESPEARE: *(Getting fired up.)* Yes. That. I want to write about that.

I want to knock on people's hearts. Show them something real.

Beat.

SHAKESPEARE: I... never went to university.

EMILIA: I know.

SHAKESPEARE: A little Latin, even less Greek.

It's a bad look for a writer.

EMILIA: Yup, it's ridiculous.

I'm mocked for being too schooled, and you for not being enough.

SHAKESPEARE: Two outcasts, then.

EMILIA: ...Sure

SHAKESPEARE: A match made in heaven!

EMILIA: Maybe.

Minus the attitude.

SHAKESPEARE: Yours or mine?

They laugh. A shared look of recognition.

SHAKESPEARE: Emilia... I'm serious.

Collaborate with me.

I think I need your mind.

EMILIA: You want me to...YES, absolutely!

And...would you take a look at my poems?

I think I need yours.

SHAKESPEARE: Yes, absolutely!

A swell in the music, she looks back towards the stage, excited for the show.

He is still lost in thought.

EMILIA: It's about to begin!

SHAKESPEARE: I want to create something of substance, something significant, you know?

EMILIA: I know!

SHAKESPEARE: Something true. Something lasting.

EMILIA: Yes!

SHAKESPEARE: That holds a mirror up to—

EMILIA: Shhh, here they come. WHOA! Look at those costumes!
What's the play about tonight?

SHAKESPEARE: Fairies.

Contrapuntal Fugue 2

"Two melodic voices, independent but related harmonically"

> *Evening in a secluded courtyard, EMILIA is cradling his script to her chest, waiting for him in anticipation. SHAKESPEARE arrives, holding a small stack of her poetry.*

EMILIA: You.

SHAKESPEARE: You.

I haven't slept since we last met.

EMILIA: A bit dramatic, no?

SHAKESPEARE: Everything is a bit dramatic, in the right context.

I've been writing, a lot.

My mind is racing faster than I can get words on the page.

It's like… I'm on the edge of something.

(He sees the script in her hands.)

You read my play!!

EMILIA: I did!

Will…You wrote *us* in here, didn't you?

SHAKESPEARE: It's possible.

EMILIA: I know you did.

SHAKESPEARE: I did.

EMILIA: "O God that I were a man, I would eat his heart in the marketplace."

SHAKESPEARE: Sounds like you.

EMILIA: Think people will know?

SHAKESPEARE: I hope they will.

Beat.

EMILIA: And what about mine? Did you read?

SHAKESPEARE: Every verse.

EMILIA: *(Expectantly.)* And?

SHAKESPEARE: Your writing is…intense.

Very bold.

EMILIA: Is it?

SHAKESPEARE: A lot of exclamation marks.

EMILIA: I'm expressive.

SHAKESPEARE: "Greatness is no sure frame to build upon,

No worldly treasure can assure that place.

God makes both even the Cottage and the Throne.

All worldly honours, there, are counted base!"

EMILIA: …is it too political?

SHAKESPEARE: Where did you learn to write like that?

EMILIA: I could ask you the same question!

SHAKESPEARE: It's all very powerful.

It's a lot to take in.

EMILIA: A lot… Too much?

SHAKESPEARE: Well, you know, *maybe*, for some people.

Beat.

EMILIA: Do you think it's good enough?

SHAKESPEARE: Good enough for what?

EMILIA: … Good enough to publish.

SHAKESPEARE: Uh… Emilia.

Women don't really write professionally.

EMILIA: I know.

SHAKESPEARE: Especially not poetry about…

Usually it's something religious.

EMILIA: I know.

SHAKESPEARE: Like a Bible translation or a Christmas hymn.

EMILIA: Yup.

               And "looking different" definitely won't help. I know.

               Is it good enough to get past all of that?

SHAKESPEARE: I think…you'd have to find the right advocate.

               But even then, Emilia…it'd be a shot in the dark.

EMILIA: The right advocate… Okay.

               Does anyone come to mind?

SHAKESPEARE: I—I'm happy to look into it for you.

EMILIA: What about your patron, the Earl of Southhampton?

SHAKESPEARE: *(He bristles.)* Wriothesley? No.

               We had a falling-out.

               We'll find you someone else. Someone better.

EMILIA: I know I can do it.

               I want to get so good they can't say no.

SHAKESPEARE: You are something else.

                              Beat.

               I read the book you gave me. Boccaccio.

EMILIA: And? What did you think?

SHAKESPEARE: It gave me an idea for a new play.

               Could you take a look?

EMILIA: Sure!

                 He pulls out the manuscript and hands it to her.

SHAKESPEARE: It's very Italian.

                 It's very *passionate.*

EMILIA: Sounds about right.

SHAKESPEARE: It's a love story.

EMILIA: A love story!

SHAKESPEARE: Young love.

EMILIA: Aww! How does it end?

SHAKESPEARE: Like all young love stories. Badly.

EMILIA: Yikes.

SHAKESPEARE: Can you make sure Juliet feels... real?

EMILIA: Okay!

SHAKESPEARE: I want her to feel as real as you.

                 As real as... *this!*

                 He squeezes her arms.

EMILIA: As real as—?

                 He kisses her, spontaneously.
                 They share a charged, suspended moment.

EMILIA: Oh…

                 Well, this will end badly.

                 She kisses him back, passionately.

ACT II

Tonal Memory

"Ability to recall and hold in your mind a previously sounded tone"

> *Music. EMILIA is reading* Romeo and Juliet *and is moved by the ending.*
>
> *A memory comes to her.*

EMILIA: You know, I visited Italy once.

With half the Bassano clan.

I still remember the smell. The warmth of the cobblestones baking in the sun.

There's one specific place… it's so clear it's like I'm still there.
We're in Bassano, the town my family got its name from.
It's just north of Venice.

I'm sitting in the main piazza by a babbling fountain.
There are two shops on either side of the square, and a large painted fresco covering the biggest building at the centre.

One shop, an apothecary, has a sign with a Black man's face on it, painted after the man who runs it, it's called The Moor.

His name's Montano. He's a sweet old man who now walks with a cane.
He knew my grandfather well. They used to play music together.

The shop across the way has a stag sign hanging above it.
It's owned by the Otellos. They're merchants. They trade leather for musical instruments with my family back in England.

Everyone is in there talking business, but I stay outside and wander towards the giant fresco.

Right at the centre, there's this beautiful naked woman. Her arms are outstretched. She's holding a torch. They call her "The Naked Truth."

She's flanked on both sides by woodwinds and strings, goats and monkeys.
She's also right between two sets of window shutters, called "gelosias." Jealousies. They can be closed on her during the day, to keep her hidden. Or opened up to reveal her in all of her glory at night.

The men in town deliberately keep her shuttered most of the time.
There was a worry she'd be too distracting.

Antiphony

"Two musical phrases in opposition"

> *Mid-dramaturgical session, late night, backstage. They are surrounded by ink, paper and two empty bottles of wine. As they fight for their ideas, it's playful in spirit. They have been arguing for some time and are in the throes of it.*

SHAKESPEARE: *(Drawing a line in the sand.)* No No No No NO. No way.

EMILIA: Yes!

SHAKESPEARE: My God, woman, no.

EMILIA: Yes!

SHAKESPEARE: Terrible idea. Cannot put that on stage.

EMILIA: I'm telling you, you can.

SHAKESPEARE: I write a line, you challenge it.

You fight me on everything.

You'd fight me on whether the sun was the sun.

EMILIA: I would if you were wrong.

SHAKESPEARE: Burbage is never going to want to play this part.

EMILIA: You'll find someone else.

He's a pompous ass anyway. He just wants to act with himself.

SHAKESPEARE: The character has no personality. He's a sad sack.

He needs a battle. A hero's quest. Something.

EMILIA: It's a heroine's quest! That's what you wrote! It's amazing!

SHAKESPEARE: Nope. It's crap.

Two problems. One: Why on earth does she like him, huh?

What makes him so special?

EMILIA: He's a good, earnest guy. There's nothing wrong with that!
He's the harmony, she's the melody. It works.

SHAKESPEARE: *(A flash of insight.)* OH OH OH!!
What if I get him to wrestle someone shirtless, right off the top.
Set him up as a sweaty hunk: one look and she's smitten.

EMILIA: Ugh, that's so cheesy.

SHAKESPEARE: People like cheese. Trust me.

EMILIA: Fine. Wrestling match.

SHAKESPEARE: Okay. Then, problem number two: the whole power dynamic is off.

EMILIA: What? No. Why?

SHAKESPEARE: She's in pants for too long.

EMILIA: What if she likes the pants?! What if she can speak her truth from the pants.

SHAKESPEARE: ...He's gotta be a bit dense, no?

EMILIA: He's a young man in love.

SHAKESPEARE: So that automatically makes him dense?

EMILIA: What were you like at eighteen?

SHAKESPEARE: …I knocked up an older woman who kept glancing at me at church.

They share a look.

SHAKESPEARE: *(Concedes.)* Dense.

EMILIA: Trust me on this. She's delightful. Take a risk. Please?

SHAKESPEARE: Fine. FINE. As you like it.

Pause. EMILIA smiles mischievously.

SHAKESPEARE: What?

EMILIA: You didn't see my notes on the monologue?

SHAKESPEARE: You made NOTES?

EMILIA: Page 42.

SHAKESPEARE: *(Flips through a few pages and reads.)* What did you do— Nooooo!

No no. Nope. No way.

EMILIA: Oh yeah.

SHAKESPEARE: No! It's just not what a woman would say!

EMILIA: And why not?

SHAKESPEARE: I don't know. It's just too…

EMILIA: What?

SHAKESPEARE: Ugh…I don't really want to say it.

EMILIA: Oh nonono. Say it.

SHAKESPEARE: ......Wise...

EMILIA: Wow.

SHAKESPEARE: What?

EMILIA: Wooow.

SHAKESPEARE: Stop.

EMILIA: You're such a product of the way things are.

SHAKESPEARE: Hey!

EMILIA: Are you sure this has nothing to do with the fact that the only women you've seen on stage are twelve-year-old boys?

SHAKESPEARE: Is this about Sam? He's a good kid.

EMILIA: Nothing against Sam. He's a great kid.

                   But women are on stage everywhere else in Europe, you know that, right?

                   GOD. I would love to be up there.

SHAKESPEARE: You'd be a terror. You'd boss all the other actors around.

                   Beat. Idea.

EMILIA: Okay. Let's try something.

                   Gimme your pants.

SHAKESPEARE: What??

EMILIA: You heard me. It's an experiment.
                   Let's swap.

SHAKESPEARE: *(Uncertain.)* Uhhh..

EMILIA: *(Ordering.)* Eh! Drop 'em.

There is an exchange of clothing.

He wears her skirt, she wears his pants.

EMILIA: Now, you are me and I am you.

SHAKESPEARE: ...I think the magic of theatre can only go so far.

EMILIA: You're a woman. Put yourself in the mindset. And you're going to woo me.

> *Shakespeare uncomfortably sways his hips as he tries to get into it... He runs his hands up his thighs, waist, chest, and tries to create some cleavage.*

> *A beat.*

> *They both burst out laughing.*

EMILIA: Seriously!?

SHAKESPEARE: I don't know!... I just... I don't know how to act, or feel woman...ly.

EMILIA: Whatever you feel would be what I would feel.

We're made of the same stuff, Will, okay?

So how would you woo me?

> *Beat.*

SHAKESPEARE: I'd make me a willow cabin at your gate
And call upon my soul within the house.
Write loyal cantons of contemned love
And sing them loud even in the dead of night.
Halloo your name to the reverberate hills
And make the babbling gossip of the air
Cry out Emilia!

Pause.

SHAKESPEARE: How did I do?

EMILIA: ... that was really good.

SHAKESPEARE: I did good?

EMILIA: ...too good. Yes.

SHAKESPEARE: I passed?

EMILIA: Definitely.

Beat.

EMILIA: ...How do you do it?

SHAKESPEARE: What?

EMILIA: You know what. It's like it drips from you.

SHAKESPEARE: It doesn't. I never know what to say in real life.

Plays are...easier.

EMILIA: *(Both turned on and jealous.)* I hate you, you know that?

SHAKESPEARE: That good, eh?

She nods.

EMILIA: Show me.

SHAKESPEARE: You want me to....

EMILIA: Teach me *how*...

A bit of role-play as she deepens her voice and strikes a pose to play "the man." Amazed, he plays along, assuming the role of "the woman."

EMILIA: Teach me. My muse. My goddess. My nymph.

SHAKESPEARE: Oh my.

EMILIA: Endow me with your music.

SHAKESPEARE: Oh.

EMILIA: And fill me.

SHAKESPEARE: OH OH OH!

EMILIA: Top full. From the crown to the toe.

SHAKESPEARE: You make me blush!

EMILIA: Let me drink from the fountain of your knowledge.

SHAKESPEARE: Why, sir!

EMILIA: Too much?

SHAKESPEARE: Not at all.

                Shall we "counterpoint" this somewhere more private, milord?

                He curtsies.

EMILIA: What you will, milady.

                She bows.

                She starts taking off the pants.

SHAKESPEARE: ...no no. No no no. Leave the pants on.

                They swell into each other. There is a rapture of delight, a flurry of laughter, perhaps a game of dress up or dress down. Perhaps the billowing of sheets. A hint of Anthony and Cleopatra. It is playful, sensual and meaningful.

Sacred Polyphony

"Heavenly harmony."

> We find them in each other's arms, backstage. Nestled in a mound of tangled sheets and costumes.

EMILIA: She messes him up.

SHAKESPEARE: Just from talking?

EMILIA: Just from meeting. The world changes for both of them.

The Queen of Sheba hears about King Solomon's wisdom.

She's pretty whip-smart herself, so she's intrigued.

She wants to see this "wise" guy.

It was supposed to be a diplomatic mission.

But when they meet, they lock eyes and time swells.

Two souls start resonating at the exact same pitch, creating a harmony so sweet you can't tell the notes apart.

(Outstretching an arm to the sky.) So sweet, it's as if heaven opens and gives them both a glimpse of the everlasting.

SHAKESPEARE: Whoa.

EMILIA: I mean, you don't truly know someone until you know them biblically.

SHAKESPEARE: …Nice.

EMILIA: So he can't get her out of his head, and he writes a bunch of love songs about her which become the Songs of Solomon.

SHAKESPEARE: So that's your favourite Bible story?

EMILIA: Yeah. It feels more… equal. You know?

                That's the one I'd write about, if I absolutely had to…
                I always liked it.
                (Change of gears.) Did you read my poems?

SHAKESPEARE: No! I haven't gotten the chance, I've been caught in my head with this next play.

EMILIA: Are you kidding me?

SHAKESPEARE: I will soon! Did you read mine?

EMILIA: Yeah!

SHAKESPEARE: What do you think?

EMILIA: They're outstanding!

                He beams.

SHAKESPEARE: *"Outstanding."* Nice.

EMILIA: But.

SHAKESPEARE: But?

EMILIA: They're also all about everything coming to an end.

SHAKESPEARE: It's a rhetorical trope. You know, the sands of time, impermanence…

EMILIA: Yeah, but it's like… everywhere!

SHAKESPEARE: It is?

EMILIA: So why is this so important to you?
                  The ravages of time, precious beauty
                  slipping through your— ....Oh!

SHAKESPEARE: What?

EMILIA: *(Gently.)* Oh. No, no, it's okay. I get it!

SHAKESPEARE: ... what. What?

EMILIA: You're going bald.

SHAKESPEARE: Wh— Hey! No. NO. ...I am not bald.

EMILIA: You know I'd love you with or without hair,
                  right?

SHAKESPEARE: No, I'm not, that's not at all what the, no.

EMILIA: *(Diverting)* So, there are a few poems in here
                  that are really over the top.

SHAKESPEARE: There are??

EMILIA: Let's get to the bottom of this.
                  Who's this Fair Youth?

SHAKESPEARE: No, no names.
                  I keep it anonymous so people can focus on
                  the work and not try to—

EMILIA: Henry Wriothesley, the Earl of Southampton.

SHAKESPEARE: ......how, how did you....?

EMILIA: "My master-mistress."
                  Flowy feminine hair?
                  It's so obvious it's him.
                  That guy is way too fond of his freaking hair.

SHAKESPEARE: So...you know him?

EMILIA: A bit.

SHAKESPEARE: *(Suddenly suspicious.)* You're close?

EMILIA: Not in the least. We were neighbours
                   growing up.
                   (Point blank.) ...Are you in love with the Earl
                   of Southampton?

SHAKESPEARE: What? No.

EMILIA: Your sonnets kinda say so.

SHAKESPEARE: No. He was the money.
                   He got me started as a proper writer.

EMILIA: And...?

SHAKESPEARE: I don't know.
                   The plague hit and theatres closed right
                   when I was finally getting some traction.
                   It was brutal... He helped me publish some
                   poems instead. Said it would boost my
                   reputation.

EMILIA: Did it?

SHAKESPEARE: I think so. Things took off from there.
                   He's the reason I have a career.

EMILIA: And the reason you pierced your ear.

SHAKESPEARE: ...No.

EMILIA: It's me, Will. You can tell me.

                   Pause.

SHAKESPEARE: You don't even seem fazed by the... idea.

EMILIA: Honestly, I'm much more concerned about
                   your taste in men.
                   Why WRIOTHESLEY? He's such a—

SHAKESPEARE: Dick?

EMILIA: Yeah.

SHAKESPEARE: He believed in me.
I think I liked who I was around him.
I felt, I don't know...
(He tries to physicalize the feeling of expansiveness.) Bigger?
But it was true. It was real... I think?
...I don't really want to talk about it anymore.

EMILIA: My first poems were about the Countess that schooled me.
She chose me. She believed in me.
I was so terrified she'd change her mind one day.
I was in awe...but it was more than that.
I was in love with her.
I think?
I'm not sure what it means either.

Pause.

EMILIA: At least my benefactor was kind to me.
This guy clearly had you whipped.

SHAKESPEARE: No.

EMILIA: Definitely whipped.

SHAKESPEARE: No. Can we drop this?

EMILIA: Sure. Okay.

Pause.

EMILIA: So, where is Wriostheley now, anyway?

SHAKESPEARE: In the Tower, for treason.
I'm taking care of his cat.

Extempore

"Free performance of a musical passage"

> *Music. They're both composing, in separate places, at the same time. Perhaps crisscrossing paths as they speak, unaware of the other.*

SHAKESPEARE: In the old age, Black was not counted fair,

EMILIA: Here is a lover that appears so fair,

SHAKESPEARE: Or if it were, it bore not beauty's name;

EMILIA: So sweet, so lovely in his lover's sight,

SHAKESPEARE: But now is Black beauty's successive heir,

EMILIA: That unto Snow we may his face compare,

SHAKESPEARE: And beauty, slander'd with a bastard shame:

EMILIA: His cheeks like scarlet and his eyes so bright

SHAKESPEARE: Therefore my mistress' brows are Raven Black,

EMILIA: Black as a Raven in her blackest hue;

SHAKESPEARE: Her Eyes so suited, and they mourners seem

EMILIA: Yea, he is constant and his words are true,

SHAKESPEARE: At such who, not born fair, no beauty lack,

EMILIA: His Lips like Lilies dropping down pure myrrh,

SHAKESPEARE: Slandering creation with a false esteem:

EMILIA: Whose love above all worlds we do prefer.

SHAKESPEARE: Yet so they mourn, becoming of their woe,

That every tongue says beauty should look so.

They meet excitedly and exchange poetry.

They read, smile back to each other.
He hastily grabs his jacket, hands her back her poem and leaves.
She stays behind holding both works, one in each hand.

Her eyes hover back to his poem.
She places his on top of hers.

Dissonance

"A tension or clash which moves away from stability"

A covered passageway outside Court. A hasty meeting.

EMILIA: Hi.

SHAKESPEARE: You.

I've been looking for you, where were you yesterday?

EMILIA: Shhh. Just... please keep your voice down. Were you followed?

SHAKESPEARE: What?

EMILIA: Were you followed?

SHAKESPEARE: No, I don't think so.

EMILIA: I don't have much time.

SHAKESPEARE: What's going on? Why haven't I seen you in weeks?

EMILIA: They're making arrangements for my wedding.

SHAKESPEARE: WEDDING? Wait, what? When?

EMILIA: Next week.

SHAKESPEARE: Next week?!

EMILIA: It's kind of a last-minute thing.

SHAKESPEARE: To who?

EMILIA: Alphonse Lanier.

SHAKESPEARE: The freaking flautist??

EMILIA: Yeah.

SHAKESPEARE: I thought you couldn't stand him.

EMILIA: He's my cousin, of course I can't stand him.

SHAKESPEARE: Then why would you ever say yes?
               Emilia, it's you: fight!
               Don't let them dictate your life.

EMILIA: Will. I'm pregnant.

SHAKESPEARE: You're...

EMILIA: Turns out an open mistress is one thing but a pregnant open mistress is another.

SHAKESPEARE: *(Still processing.)* You're...

EMILIA: They're marrying me off to avoid any scandal.
               The Lord Chamberlain's already paid Alphonse a ton of money to keep his mouth shut.

SHAKESPEARE: *(Panic setting in.)* Em, don't do it! Don't go through with it!

Alphonse is a drunken lout. You'll be miserable.

EMILIA: It's that or the street, Will. They're casting me out of Court.

SHAKESPEARE: There has to be another way! What can I...?

What if you escape?

EMILIA: Where?

...Alone?

He has no answer. She bolsters herself.

EMILIA: No. I have to do this.

It's the only way to salvage the bit of reputation I might still have left.

She tries to leave.

SHAKESPEARE: Wait. Wait!
Let's figure something out.
I can't just lose you. Em, I need you!
How do we speak? How do we meet?

EMILIA: You don't understand, people are already talking.
If they see me with you it'll make it so much worse.

SHAKESPEARE: The willow tree.

EMILIA: What?

SHAKESPEARE: The willow tree in Bishopsgate cemetery. The one you said looked sad because of its hollow trunk.

EMILIA: What about it?

SHAKESPEARE: Leave your letters in the hollow. I will too.

EMILIA: This isn't a play, Will.

SHAKESPEARE: It's a way for us to stay connected.

EMILIA: I have to go.

               She's on her way out but he stops her.

SHAKESPEARE: Emilia. Wait.

               They look at each other. The real question.

SHAKESPEARE: Is it? Is it...? ... I need to know....

EMILIA: *(It hurts that he even had to ask.)* It won't— ...
                it won't matter.

SHAKESPEARE: Of course it will.

EMILIA: *(At a loss.)* Will...

SHAKESPEARE: Tell me.

EMILIA: Would it really change anything, if it was?

SHAKESPEARE: ...I don't know.

               His hesitancy hurts. She recoils.

EMILIA: Some things are better left in the dark.

               She leaves.

ACT III

Monody

"A single melodic line"

> *Music. EMILIA's monologue is the writing of her letter.*

EMILIA: Dear Will,
You were right.
Alphonse is a raging drunk. And a terrible flautist.
It's been... an adjustment, to say the least.
Silver lining: he turned soldier.
He heard there was money to be made in the navy and set sail.
It does make for quieter nights.

> *She touches her stomach*

I'm scared, Will. I miss everything. I miss...
(you)

> *She doubts. Instead.*

Did you read my poems? What did you think?

> *She leaves the letter in the tree.*

Tension Chord

"Dissonance within the chord, creating tension because all of the tones want to go somewhere else."

Evening. She's been waiting for him somewhere secluded. He arrives.

EMILIA: Hey!

SHAKESPEARE: Hey.

EMILIA: What did you think?

SHAKESPEARE: What? About what?

EMILIA: My poems!

SHAKESPEARE: Oh. Yeah, they were good.

EMILIA: Oh God, they were shit.

SHAKESPEARE: No, they weren't shit.

EMILIA: Then why aren't you saying more?

SHAKESPEARE: What do you want me to say?

EMILIA: Anything!

SHAKESPEARE: I liked them! A lot!

EMILIA: I'm gonna need more than that.

SHAKESPEARE   Whoa, okay whoa, I just got here. Can we stop for a second? Hi.

EMILIA: Hi…

SHAKESPEARE: Sorry. I'm all…

The Queen picked Fletcher's play over mine.

EMILIA: So?

SHAKESPEARE: I can't get it out of my head.

EMILIA: It's just one play, one time.

SHAKESPEARE: That's how it starts, you know?

EMILIA: …okay.

SHAKESPEARE: I'm so tense, Em. Each time a play's successful, I panic about the next one.
I keep bracing myself…expecting I'll be denounced for some great scandal, or accused of treason, or get jumped coming home from the bar.

Do you remember Julius Caesar? You had sent me a bit for Portia?

EMILIA: (*Nods.*) "Dwell I but in the suburbs of your good pleasure?"

SHAKESPEARE: I botched the ending. I had to rush to meet the deadline.

I accidentally wrote three honour suicides, back to back, without realizing it.

EMILIA: (*She winces.*) Three?

SHAKESPEARE: Three.

EMILIA: That's overkill.

SHAKESPEARE: You're telling me.

By the time it got to the last actor impaling himself on his sword, the audience was howling with laughter. We couldn't even hear the dialogue.

And I went along with it! …I watched myself laughing with them like an idiot, just happy to have dodged a flop.

I miss this. I miss *us*. I feel like I wrote better when you were around.

EMILIA: ...okay.

SHAKESPEARE: I'm confiding in you here.

EMILIA: I don't know what you want me to say...

SHAKESPEARE: Anything.

EMILIA: I'm so sorry things are going well?

SHAKESPEARE: Jeez, Emilia.

Pause.

SHAKESPEARE: ...are you okay?

EMILIA stares at him.

SHAKESPEARE: What—what's going on?

EMILIA: Will...are you serious?

SHAKESPEARE: Hey hey hey. Come on.

EMILIA: It's over... My life is ruined.

SHAKESPEARE: It's not! It's going to be okay. It will.

EMILIA: And meanwhile, everyone's flocking into theatres to hear the next "Shakespeare" play.

SHAKESPEARE: Why... why aren't you happy for us?

EMILIA: You mean happy for you!

SHAKESPEARE: Emilia. You're my muse. My music. We're in this together.

I don't know how else to tell you that.

EMILIA: We're in this together?

SHAKESPEARE: Yes!

EMILIA: We're in this together?

SHAKESPEARE: Yes!

EMILIA: Then can you help me find a patron?

SHAKESPEARE: How about your Countess? Or some of the ladies of the court?

EMILIA: No answer.
I've written to every woman in power I know.
I wrote to the Queen herself. Nothing.
People I knew as almost equals, won't look me in the eye when I pass them in the street.
I *need* this, I need to find a way to publish, Will.
And you're the one around powerful people now…So can you help me? Be my supporter! Help me get my name out there!

SHAKESPEARE: Emilia, I'm here, I'm here as much as I can be…I don't know how much more I can… You're…you're suffocating me.

EMILIA :   I'm…… what?

SHAKESPEARE: No, Em, I …Look. Let's work on your stuff together! I can help with that.
Just give this time to blow over.
That courtly life… who's in favour, who's not. It's a game. It'll pass. It will.

EMILIA: This is not a game. It's my life.
It's my story.
It's my body.
It's a price you can't understand.

SHAKESPEARE: I can try to.

The baby kicks.

EMILIA: OH.

SHAKESPEARE: What?

EMILIA: She kicked. She kicked! That's the first time she...

SHAKESPEARE: She?

EMILIA: ...I'm hoping for a she.

                    Beat.

SHAKESPEARE: Can— Can I feel it?

> *He places his hand on her stomach. The baby kicks again.*
> *They both feel it. They share the wonder in laughter...but as their eyes meet, EMILIA's smile fades. They share a wistful look.*
> *She then makes a decision, and places a stack of her writing in his hands.*
> *An invitation.*

Imitative Polyphony

"Simultaneous musical lines, similar in shape and sound"

> *He is reading her work and making notes, actively trying to help.*
> *Perhaps a reversal of the first dramaturgical session except now he's the dramaturge and she's the writer.*

SHAKESPEARE: No. No. Emilia.
                    You can't write that. Not in your own voice.

EMILIA: Why not?

SHAKESPEARE: No wonder no one's answering you back!

EMILIA: It's what I believe. I've got to be able to speak my truth, no?

SHAKESPEARE: You have to be very careful what you write. Your words can be used against you.

EMILIA: Hey, I used to read some of this at Court. They supported—

SHAKESPEARE: They weren't supporting you, they *tolerated* you.

They entertained the notion of you. But it's an entirely different thing to—

EMILIA: Is that what you think of me?

SHAKESPEARE: Of course not.
(*Beat, he tries again gently.*) Listen…this whole thing, it's a delicate balance… You have to have a deft hand.

EMILIA: So, is that what success *is*? Smuggling poetry between dick jokes and propaganda?

SHAKESPEARE: Yes. If it sells.

She crumples. Pause.

SHAKESPEARE: (*Reads.*) "For well we know this world is but a stage
Where all do play their parts, and must be gone."

EMILIA: What about it?

SHAKESPEARE: A bit derivative, no? "All the world's a stage, and all the men and women merely players…"?

EMILIA: I came up with that.

SHAKESPEARE: Nope. I'm pretty sure I did.

EMILIA: Nope. Pretty sure it was me.

SHAKESPEARE: How about we chalk it up to "subliminal influence"?

EMILIA: Sure... But who is influencing whom?

SHAKESPEARE: We probably came up with it together.
No big deal, we're collaborators. Like with Middleton and Fletcher. You're in this with me. It's the same thing.

EMILIA: But my name can't be on it.

SHAKESPEARE: ... that's true.

EMILIA: It's off the record.
It's...It's going to be like I never existed.

SHAKESPEARE: No. Come on, you're being dramatic.

EMILIA: I want my name on what I write.

SHAKESPEARE: Emilia, what you're striving for... it's utopic.
But it's also a dead end.
Why keep throwing yourself against a wall?

EMILIA: To make a mark.

> *Pause.*
> *SHAKESPEARE begins packing up his things. He stops, gathers himself.*

SHAKESPEARE: ...Can we please talk about THIS? *(He references her growing belly.)*

EMILIA: What is there to say?

> *Pause.*
> *He finishes packing up.*

SHAKESPEARE: I'm heading back to Stratford for a few weeks... Hamnet's birthday.
He looks like me, the older he gets... it's hard.

The longer I'm gone, the less I know how to be around them all.

EMILIA nods.

SHAKESPEARE: Write to me, okay?

EMILIA: …They'll be so happy to see you.

SHAKESPEARE: I'll send you what I end up working on.

They've commissioned me for something else next month and I've got nothing.

EMILIA: …You'll come up with something, you always do.

Beat.
She rises with slight effort.

SHAKESPEARE: It's mine.
Is it? …It is. Isn't it?

Beat.

EMILIA: Of course it is.

SHAKESPEARE: What are we going to do?

A breath, as she holds his gaze.

EMILIA: Nothing.
We do nothing.

Deceptive Cadence

"The cradle of tonality...with an unexpected final note."

> *Music. EMILIA goes to the willow tree. But there's no letter from SHAKESPEARE.*

EMILIA: The space between our meetings gets longer and longer.
I wonder if you're avoiding me too.
Like everyone else.

You sometimes share your plays with me.
In what feels like an afterthought.
And they're...good.
They're so good.
I don't have anything to contribute.

You had asked me to send you what I've been writing.

> *She pulls out some pages she was planning on putting in the tree. She scans them... and then changes her mind.*

I can't bring myself to tell you how much I've written and torn up.
Nothing sticks because nothing compares.

Until something does.

Minim

"Half-note rest"

> *Music. We find EMILIA with her daughter bundled in her arms. SHAKESPEARE arrives and is moved at the sight. He approaches and she offers for him to hold her. He takes the baby in his arms. She watches him.*

EMILIA: Odyllia.

SHAKESPEARE: Odyllia... that's lovely.
                I don't think I've ever heard that name before.

EMILIA: She has your eyes.

SHAKESPEARE: She has your nose.

> *Pause. They are both overcome with emotion.*

SHAKESPEARE: ... Emilia... I... won't be able to —

EMILIA: I know.

Tacet

"The performer is to be silent. They are not to play"

> *Music. EMILIA is alone. Cradling her bundle.*

EMILIA: Odyllia.

I loved her more than myself. More than you.
And for a moment there it felt like it would be enough.

That maybe this was what it took.
This is what it could all be about.
Making the world better for her.
Writing for her.
Playing music for her...

> *The music stops. She stops.*
> *Slowly, she begins to unravel the bundle as*
> *she speaks until there is nothing left.*

It happened so fast.

She barely let me get to know her.
Her giggle, her giant blue-eyed stare.
The gentle sound of her breathing as she slept.
Her smell.

> *She smells the loose fabric.*

Grief seems to fill the room up with her loss...
How cruel to leave just as she had arrived.
...

There is no word for a parent who loses a child.

Staccato Crescendo

"A sharp and disconnected swell"

> *EMILIA is waiting by the willow tree. He*
> *arrives.*
> *They take each other in for a moment, at a*
> *loss, overwhelmed.*
> *He breaks the silence.*

SHAKESPEARE: I came as soon as I could.

EMILIA nods.

SHAKESPEARE: I'm sorry.

EMILIA: I wrote to you so many times... You never wrote back.

SHAKESPEARE: No, no, I wanted to. I was going to. I just couldn't find a... There was a lot for me to deal with.

EMILIA: ...I can't even look at you.

SHAKESPEARE: Emilia, it was complicated. I tried. I did. But—

EMILIA: I needed you and you weren't there.

SHAKESPEARE: I'm sorry, Em.

EMILIA: That's the *least* I hoped you could—

SHAKESPEARE: Hamnet died.

Pause.

SHAKESPEARE: It's been...
I went home to organize the funeral for my son.
My wife is distraught. My daughters won't talk to me.
I've been absent for too long.
I wasn't there when it happened, Em.
I wasn't there, either.

> *They are both at a loss. He is barely holding it together.*
> *She holds him.*
> *The two cling to each other in their gulf of grief.*

SHAKESPEARE: I'm so sorry, Emilia.

But then, something is off. She stiffens and pulls away.

EMILIA: Did her death mean less?

SHAKESPEARE: Em.

EMILIA: Did Odyllia mean less to you?

SHAKESPEARE: *(Lost, distraught.)* No. No!

EMILIA: *(Incredulous, almost to herself.)* You never wrote back.

SHAKESPEARE: My family needed me.

EMILIA: Your real family needed you.

SHAKESPEARE: You know that's not true.

EMILIA: *(A cold realization.)* I have no claim to anything real.
Not you, not your work, not mine.
She was ours, Will.
She was something we created together.
She was real.

SHAKESPEARE: Of course she was real. What are you talking about?

EMILIA: But the shadow of a shadow.

SHAKESPEARE: Emilia. Stop. Please.
We're going to get through this together.

EMILIA: How can you even say that?
You've made it abundantly clear, there is no "we."
There never was. They're just words, words, words.

SHAKESPEARE: ...I...
I don't know what to say....

EMILIA: Maybe it's for the better. Another lost little girl drowning in a world of men.

SHAKESPEARE: Stop that.

EMILIA: What a relief for you... eh? That your bastard child didn't survive.

SHAKESPEARE: EMILIA!

EMILIA: Thank God *that* potential scandal can now be buried.
                 Wouldn't want to *suffocate* you any more than I already have.

SHAKESPEARE: Emilia!!! What the hell? WHAT—What do I do?
                 What do you want me to do??

EMILIA: *(Fuck off.)* Just go write.

ACT IV

Fermata

"A single note held longer than its usual duration"

> *EMILIA is holding a manuscript: it's Shakespeare's new play...Hamlet. All emotions are jumbled together. Flashes of awe, pain, tenderness, envy, rage. But there's no denying: this is his chef d'oeuvre.*

EMILIA:

Hamnet and Odyllia. You wrote them a play. What you wrote...

I have no words for what you wrote.
Is this.... is this what *genius* is? Why does it hurt?

...words don't taste the same.

What was I fighting so hard for?
What do I...?
Where do I belong?

> *She progressively pulls out everything she has ever written and scatters it on the floor. Music starts to slowly build... louder, more frenetic.*
> *A kind of exalted frustration.*
>
> *Suddenly, a thought comes.*
>
> *She pulls out her grandfather's Bible. Plops the tome down next to her. And starts writing.*

Sostenuto

"Sustained musical passage where each note swells beyond its normal value"

> *They are at SHAKESPEARE's apartment. They've been trying to rekindle their conversational ease but there's too much between them now. They are catching up. A silence, mid-awkward conversation.*

SHAKESPEARE: So, I um... I got a family crest.

EMILIA: Hey, congrats! You're a bone fide gentleman now.
"Sir William." How does it feel?

SHAKESPEARE: Not so different, I guess.
I bought a house. In Stratford.

EMILIA: Oh boy. You must be a celebrity back home.

SHAKESPEARE: Not really. Nobody reads.
But... yes, they know I've been "successful."
It's a big house.

EMILIA: Okay...

SHAKESPEARE: Second largest in town.

EMILIA: Sounds to me like you made it.

SHAKESPEARE: *(Shrugs.)* I don't know.

> *Beat.*

EMILIA: Did you read the poem I sent you?

SHAKESPEARE: I did.

> *Pause.*

SHAKESPEARE: It's good.

EMILIA: ...it's good.

SHAKESPEARE: What do you want me to say?

EMILIA: No, it's good. Good. It's all good.

SHAKESPEARE: *(Gently.)* I mean...you don't need my approval.

EMILIA: ...I know.

SHAKESPEARE: Okay.

Beat.

SHAKESPEARE: I thought we could...
There's this play I'm struggling with and I would love for you to—

EMILIA: I'm sorry, Will, I won't have time.
I'm actually working on something pretty big.

SHAKESPEARE: You...are?

EMILIA: I'm rewriting the Bible.

SHAKESPEARE: You're...I'm sorry, what?

EMILIA: I'm going to play by their rules, but do it my way.
Write a religious text, while smuggling my message into scripture.

SHAKESPEARE: Uh. That's not quite what I meant when I—

EMILIA: I'm reinterpreting the Bible from the women's perspective.
Starting with Eve, then working my way up to the Virgin Mary.
Most of the women in there don't even have names.
I'm going to give each one of those women a voice.

SHAKESPEARE: Emilia....you're playing with fire.

EMILIA: Shall I read you an excerpt?

SHAKESPEARE: *(Nervous.)* Hold on. Just… Keep your voice down, okay?

EMILIA: "Man will boast of knowledge which he took
From Eve's fair hand as from a learned Book.
Then men, give us our Liberty again,
And challenge to yourselves no sovereignty,
You came not in this world without our pain,
Make that a bar against your cruelty,
Your fault being greater, why should you disdain
Us being your equals, free from tyranny?"

SHAKESPEARE: Okay. I'm going to stop you right there. *(Mustering the words.)* This country has been through so much over religion and politics. You don't want anyone suspecting you of anything.

EMILIA: They won't suspect a thing.

SHAKESPEARE: What are you calling it?

EMILIA: *Hail God, King of the Jews.*

    Beat.

SHAKESPEARE: I can't help you with this.

EMILIA: I wasn't asking for help.
You know, I finally found a patron.
He thinks I have promise.

SHAKESPEARE: *(Sharp.)* Who is he?

EMILIA: He's a fan.

SHAKESPEARE: Why don't I believe that?

EMILIA: You don't believe that I can have a fan?

SHAKESPEARE: A *male* fan.

EMILIA: You're *jealous*?!
You don't own me, you know that, right?

SHAKESPEARE: What does that have to do with it?

EMILIA: You've made it crystal clear that you can't help me.
Maybe you were never going to help me.

SHAKESPEARE: No.

EMILIA: Maybe you were hoping one day I would just drop it.

SHAKESPEARE: No.
Emilia. What you're trying to do artistically is admirable, but it's also colossal, and the work was never quite good enough to support it.

EMILIA: *(Like a dagger to the heart.)* Wow... Okay... there it is.

SHAKESPEARE: No, that's not what— You can't change the world with a poem!!

EMILIA: You hate my writing.

SHAKESPEARE: No I—...I wanted to protect you and give you time to—

EMILIA: You know, *your* work wasn't quite good enough either when I met you. But I went out of my way to help you.

SHAKESPEARE: Yes you did, and you helped me push the boundary so many times.

EMILIA: Did you though?

SHAKESPEARE: What?

EMILIA: Did you "push the boundary"?

SHAKESPEARE: Are you kidding? Of course I did.

EMILIA: Your work never really takes a stand on any issue.
                    You always toe the line and play it safe.

SHAKESPEARE: And *you* repeatedly hit people over the head with some crazy agenda.

EMILIA: At least I've never pandered to anyone.
                    I've always stayed true to what was important to me.

SHAKESPEARE: Meanwhile, I have a marketable career, and people actually enjoy what I write.

                    Silence.

EMILIA: Okay.
                    Want to know who it is?
                    Henry Wriosthesley.

SHAKESPEARE: WHAT?

EMILIA: Yeah. Doing me a favour for old time's sake.

SHAKESPEARE: No. No way.

EMILIA: Yeah, we've known each other for years. Years. Way longer than you.

SHAKESPEARE: He never told me that.

EMILIA: He wants to promote my work. *He believes in me.*

SHAKESPEARE: Stop it. Just stop.

EMILIA: He likes the Bible idea. He finds it edgy.

SHAKESPEARE: Of course he does, he's a shit-disturber.

EMILIA: He thinks art should provoke and challenge.

SHAKESPEARE: Yeah, news flash, Emilia: that's why he's always in the Tower.

EMILIA: Meanwhile, you hide yourself in your work to keep from ever having to feel anything real.

Beat.

SHAKESPEARE: *(Tentative.)* Who said that? He said that?

EMILIA: Maybe.
...You know, he really does have gorgeous hair.

SHAKESPEARE: You're trying to hurt me.

EMILIA: He called you a coward.

SHAKESPEARE: Have you fucked him?

EMILIA: And I agree with him, you are a coward.

SHAKESPEARE: Have you fucked him??!

Silence.

EMILIA: Tell me what happened with Othello.

SHAKESPEARE: What are you talking about?

EMILIA: We worked on that play for months.
You named a character after me. You let me write her a speech.

SHAKESPEARE: What about it?

EMILIA: You said opening went great.

SHAKESPEARE: It did.

EMILIA: I saw it. I never told you.

SHAKESPEARE: ...You went to Whitehall? They let you in at Court?

EMILIA: I posed as my cousin.
It involved pants, a lute and a moustache.

SHAKESPEARE: Are you serious right now?

EMILIA: I'm dead serious.
I found a way, because that story, what we wrote, it mattered.
It was important to me.
And when it got to her part, her speech... it never came.
Sweet little Desdemona just kept right on talking.
You pulled the damn speech.

SHAKESPEARE: Emilia! It's business! This whole thing is business!
It wasn't some kind of personal slight.
The show was running long.
Burbage kept pressuring me for more time for his monologue.
It was simpler just to remove it, for now.

EMILIA: "Then let men use us well: else let them know
The ills we do, their ills instruct us so."

SHAKESPEARE: She's a peripheral character and that particular speech does nothing to drive the plot of the play.

EMILIA: Oh, come on! Just admit it. You choked.

SHAKESPEARE: Do you have any idea how often I've watched friends of mine get hurt or killed for speaking up?
Randomly attacked, stabbed in bars, rotting in jail, publicly executed.
'Cause *that* is what happens!

EMILIA: (*Vehemently.*) That shit happens to my people all the time, without us even having to speak up!

Beat.

SHAKESPEARE: So what the hell are we even fighting about?

EMILIA: Everything! Everything. How you see me. What I mean to you.
Creating art. All of it, everything, all of it.

SHAKESPEARE: Come on.

EMILIA: There is no room for me in your "world view."

SHAKESPEARE: Are you kidding me?

EMILIA: You love it when people call you progressive. But you know what secretly terrifies you? It's that the man behind the work is common.

SHAKESPEARE: Wow. That's just great.

EMILIA: A simple, basic, balding, middle-aged man.

SHAKESPEARE: Again with the balding!

EMILIA: You are so conventional.
You wanted your big house and your family crest, and you got it.

SHAKESPEARE: You have never wanted me to make it, have you? / You can't stand it.

EMILIA: And you're going to get old and fat sitting within those walls. /
Priding yourself on all the wrong victories in your life.

SHAKESPEARE: Because it just reminds you what a failure your life is.

She takes it in. He immediately regrets it and tries to go to her. She leaves.

Aria

"The Masque of the Drunken Poet"

> *SHAKESPEARE is drunk. He's under her window. It's late.*

SHAKESPEARE: EMILIAAAAAAA!!! Emilia...

> ...
> "How oft when thou, my music, music play'st,
> Upon that blessed wood whose motion sounds"

> ...
> I'm sorry! I'm so sorry!
> You're right!!
> I'm a sellout. Okay?
> I'm a whore.
> I'm a whore, Immawhore-coward.
> I'm obsss- I'm obsequious.
> *Obsequious.* Nice. *(A mental note to write that down later.)*
> It. Is. Hard. Em! I do what I can.
> I'm trying, I'm always trying to open people's hearts to—...
> But I have to navigate all kinds of—...
> I... I'm sorry. Okay?
> EMILIIIIIAAAAAA!!!
> EMILIIIIIAAAAAA!!!

> *EMILIA appears at her balcony above him.*

EMILIA: What the hell are you doing. It's 2 am.

SHAKESPEARE: I'm calling on my soul within the house!

EMILIA: You're going to get us both killed.

SHAKESPEARE: "My mistress' eyes are nothing like the sun, Coral is far more red than her lips red."

EMILIA: Stop it.

SHAKESPEARE: "If snow be white, why then her breasts are
                dun,
                If hair be wires— "

EMILIA: That's enough.

SHAKESPEARE: Wait, no, listen, there's a twist!

EMILIA: I don't give a shit.

SHAKESPEARE: Emilia...
                I LOVE YOU!!! I love you. Okay?

EMILIA: *(It hurts.)* Oh…. God.

SHAKESPEARE: I do. It's you. It's all you. I need you to know
                that.
                I feel like I'm dying. I think I'm dying.

EMILIA: No one is dying for love anytime soon.

SHAKESPEARE: *(Trying to work up the courage to confess
                something.)*
                I want to tell you, I need to tell you that
                I—….
                That I—…

EMILIA: You're stinking drunk.

SHAKESPEARE: I don't know how to be without you.
                And I…I think I messed up.

EMILIA: No shit.

SHAKESPEARE: No, nooooo…You don't know. I. Messed.
                Up.

EMILIA: Will, you took exactly what you needed
                from me.

SHAKESPEARE: No shhh, just let me—I'm trying to tell you
                something—

EMILIA: Am I going to have to call a constable?

SHAKESPEARE: You're like the opposite of womankind.
                 Like a tiger. Like an evil tiger.

EMILIA: Get off my property!

SHAKESPEARE: See! See! That. *That* is why...

EMILIA: Why what? ...why what?

SHAKESPEARE: I didn't know what to do with myself, so I
                 wrote a poem about it.
                 I'm not good at... *(A gesture to mean "self-expression.")*
                 ...I always write a fucking poem about it.

EMILIA: You wrote a poem about what?

SHAKESPEARE: It's late, you should go to sleep.
                 Good night! Sweet cruelty!

Magnum Opus

"A large and important work of art that sums up an artist's life and work."

> *SHAKESPEARE's place. He is nursing a hangover. She barges in.*

EMILIA: What the hell is this?

SHAKESPEARE: ...What?

EMILIA: THIS. You published *this*?

SHAKESPEARE: ... It's a book of sonnets.

EMILIA: Yes. But what *is* it? A challenge, a
                 provocation, a smear job?

SHAKESPEARE: *(At a loss.)* It's a bestseller.

EMILIA: The woman in this is me.

SHAKESPEARE: It's all anonymous!

EMILIA: "My mistress' eyes are nothing like the sun,
Coral is far more red than her lips red,
If snow be white why then her breasts are dun
If hair be wires, black wires grow on her head—"

SHAKESPEARE: No... read until the end, there's a twist!

EMILIA: Are you serious?

SHAKESPEARE: "And yet, by heaven, I think my love as rare
As any she belied with false compare"

…

…see?…that's the twist.

Beat.

SHAKESPEARE: Emilia, no one is going to know it's you!

EMILIA: They're all calling her "The Dark Lady."
Not many of us in town, Will.

SHAKESPEARE: But it could be fiction for all they know.

EMILIA: "The Dark Lady."
If the goal was to defame me you could have at least had the courage to *name* me.

SHAKESPEARE: I wasn't trying to defame you! That's why it's anonymous!
And the publisher even liked the idea...
He said it would add an air of mystery.

EMILIA: You want to be seen as a poet so bad you're willing to expose our intimacy?

SHAKESPEARE: Emilia, look. I had no intention to publish them all.
It was only going to be a few…
But they kept pressuring me on the "box set" idea.
They wanted an arc to the whole story.

EMILIA: It's not the whole story.

SHAKESPEARE: The first poem I ever wrote to you is in there!
"Thy Black is fairest in my judgment's place.
Therefore I swear beauty herself is Black
And all they foul that thy complexion lack."

EMILIA: Yeah…and the last one too.
"For I have sworn thee fair, and thought thee bright,
Who art as black as hell, as dark as night."

SHAKESPEARE: … I—I wrote in anger.
It's a rhetorical trope.
That's not what I think of you, Em.

EMILIA: "The Dark Lady."

SHAKESPEARE: I never even wrote that! I never called you that.
You are so much more than that to me! …

A painful, uncomfortable beat.

EMILIA: Okay… Okay.
This has to happen, now.

SHAKESPEARE: Where are you going?

EMILIA: To PUBLISH my RESPONSE.
This will not be how I am remembered.
This will not be my legacy.

ACT V

Caesura

"A brief pause during which metrical time is not counted"

> *Music.*

EMILIA: I publish.

It takes me years. *Years.*
I turn my house into a school for girls. My extensive library going to good use.

And as soon as I earn enough, I head to the publishing house.

Stepping inside is overwhelming. It is deafening.
The metallic click-clacking of thousands of tiny letter blocks.
The creaking of the giant printing press.
And the smell.
The smell of freshly smacked ink on rough new paper.
It smells like what knowledge should smell like.
It smells… amazing.

I'm sweating as I hand my work over…
They're grumbling and very suspicious.
But I give them all of my earnings up front and they change their tune.

Then I wait…
It sits on someone's desk. For a year. Two.
They keep putting it off. Making excuses.
I pester, I bribe, I fight tooth and nail to get
this thing into print.

And finally… I did it.
I PUBLISHED.

She holds out her small book.

The first female professional poet on English
soil.

(*Quickly, giddily.*) I published I published
I published I published I published I
published I published!!!
…
No one's read it, though.

King James commissioned his Bible
translation the same month.
Everyone who could read, was reading that.

I don't think I sold a single copy.
But…. it *exists*.

A moment.
She places the book down.

A few months later, three constables show
up at my door to escort me to the Tower.
Like a criminal, in front of my students.

(*Almost excited at the prospect.*) It has to be my
poetry!
I'm challenging the state of things.
Someone powerful must be incensed!
Right?

She shakes her head.

Instead, news had gotten around that some "dark lady of ill repute" was teaching young girls how to fight for what they want.
...People really don't like that.

No one knew I had written anything at all.

I got sent to the Tower.
Finally got to see what all the fuss was about.
But my bail never came.

I found out my husband had squandered the very last of our money and then up and died overseas...
It was looking grim.

But then someone I hadn't seen in a while bails me out.

Bitonality

"Using two keys at the same time"

> *A small rental apartment above the Blackfriars Theatre.*
> *They are cautious with each other.*

SHAKESPEARE: Is this... will this be suitable for you?

EMILIA: Yes! Yes... it's— *(This is hard to say.)* It's incredibly generous. It's more than I can ever repay you. *(Formal.)* I'm eternally grateful. Thank you.

SHAKESPEARE: ...The Blackfriars Theatre is right down-stairs. I hope it won't be too noisy.

EMILIA: It's perfect.
I wasn't sure how I was going to—

SHAKESPEARE: I heard. I wanted to help.

> I know it doesn't make up for…
> It's the least I could do.

Beat.

EMILIA looks outside.

EMILIA: There's a willow in the courtyard.

SHAKESPEARE: There is…

Pause.

He pulls out her small book. She is speechless.

SHAKESPEARE: Emilia.
You published!! You did it!

EMILIA: That's…

SHAKESPEARE: You never told me!

EMILIA: Where did you get that?!

SHAKESPEARE: I bought it.

EMILIA: *(She is incredulous.)* You did?

SHAKESPEARE: "Men, who, forgetting that they were born of women, do, like vipers, deface the very wombs wherein they were bred."

EMILIA: *(It feels silly now.)* …God.

SHAKESPEARE: In print, Em.
I own a Bassano now.

He tenderly smells her book.
Pause.

EMILIA: I saw *The Winter's Tale*…

SHAKESPEARE: You did?

EMILIA: It was… exquisite.
It's a redemption story.

SHAKESPEARE: …yes.

EMILIA: I like that Paulina woman.

SHAKESPEARE: Oh yeah?

EMILIA: Lots of rage there.

SHAKESPEARE: She's fire.

EMILIA: "I'll use that tongue I have: if wit flow from't
As boldness from my bosom, let't not be doubted
I shall do good."

Beat, a quiet smile between them.
He offers her a manuscript.

EMILIA: What's this?

SHAKESPEARE: A play. It never got put on...
A heroine. Talented, bright and virtuous, but of low birth.
Her father dies and she's brought up by a rich Countess...
She's impossibly in love, reaching high above her rank, and incredibly determined to prove her worth through her deeds.

EMILIA: Who is she in love with?

SHAKESPEARE: *(Remorseful.)* A young man who winds up being cruel because he's too young and stupid to understand what love means.

They share a moment. He tears up. She touches him gently.

EMILIA: Girls always mature faster.

Beat.

EMILIA: *"All's Well That Ends Well."* Does it?

SHAKESPEARE: I have absolutely no idea.

EMILIA: Your company didn't like it?

SHAKESPEARE: Burbage really hated Bertram. ...And no one liked Helen either.
                     They felt she had too strong a will.

EMILIA: *(She hugs the manuscript.)* She was ahead of her time.

SHAKESPEARE: Emilia... Thank you.

Requiem

"A Mass for the Dead"

                     Music.

EMILIA: We seem to both harden and soften as we age.
                     We witness more ends and fewer beginnings.
                     We ask ourselves what will *last.*

                     "The Sands of Time"...
                     A rhetorical trope.

                     It's June, I think.

                     I'm looking out my window.

                     And...I—I'm watching your theatre burn.

                     It's the smell that catches me first... then the billowing clouds of black smoke...
                     People are gathered on both sides of the riverbanks.
                     And I know you're there.

You'd have to be there....

Your church is burning.

I don't even remember making a decision. I just launch myself towards the river, across the bridge, towards...you.

It's a scrum of people, running, shouting, crying.
I can't get any closer.
I'm scanning the crowd.
Everyone is looking up at the towering flames... but one solitary figure is facing the opposite direction, walking towards the bank of the river.

> *SHAKESPEARE appears, with his back to her.*

I don't recognize you at first.
I see an old man. Older than your age.
Hunched over.
Peering into the Thames.
Its watery depths, the laps of the waves.
As the fire rages behind you.
But then you turn around.

> *Shakespeare turns to her. They lock eyes and time swells.*
> *She speaks on his behalf.*

"I'll break my staff,
Bury it certain fathoms in the earth,
And deeper than did ever plummet sound
I'll drown my book."

> *He walks away and she is left alone.*

Music of the Spheres

"The sound the universe makes as it turns"

> *EMILIA is at SHAKESPEARE's grave.*
> *She is carrying a large stack of loosely*
> *bundled paper.*

EMILIA: You.

> *She kneels to touch the grave. She reaches*
> *in her pocket and places a pebble on his*
> *tombstone.*

Hi.

> *She looks around the church and spots the*
> *bust on the wall.*

Oh my lord. That bust.
Is that supposed to be you?
Wow…that's.
(*Gestures a bald head.*)
You know, I'm not going to say anything.
It's very nice.

I brought you something.

Your friends they…they published your
work… in Folio.
FOLIO, Will!

You know they don't bind manuscripts this
big?
It's huge.

Of course I bought it.

> *She presses it to her chest and instinctively,*
> *imperceptibly rocks it.*

A heavy bundle of loose leaves cradled
against my skin.

The weight of a lifetime.

She smells the First Folio. A beat.

So…I carefully bring it home and then I trip on my doorstep and the pages go flying and scatter across the hearth.
All of your plays merging together on my cold floor.

She carefully flips through the pages.

"Do you not know I am a woman? When I think I must speak!"
"I cannot be a man with wishing therefore I will die a woman with grieving."
"I am fire and air. I have immortal longings in me."

…Will.

… I'm in here.
Throughout.
I know that now.

There's an Emilia in *Othello*,
An Emilia in *Comedy of Errors*,
An Emilia in *Winter's Tale*,
There's an Amelius in *Julius Caesar*,
An Aemilius in *Anthony and Cleopatra*,
An Aemilius and a Bassanius in *Titus Andronicus*,
And there is a Bassanio in *The Merchant of Venice*.

I'm… *everywhere*.
You put me everywhere.

She places the Folio at his grave.
She hears music. Faint in her ear.

EMILIA: Do you hear that?

She looks around, she's alone.
But the music becomes louder, louder.
She looks up.
Her face softens. She smiles.

Music.
I hear...music.

She outstretches her arms to the sky.

...As if heaven opens.

SHAKESPEARE appears in the distance.
He beckons her to come to him.
She runs to him.
They embrace.

They disappear, together.

The end.

Historical Timeline

1539

Baptista Bassano (Emilia's father) and four of his brothers depart from Venice for England. The Bassanos were a family of Venetian court musicians who had played for the Doge of Venice. King Henry VIII had heard of their musical virtuosity and recruited them to revitalize his court. The Bassanos dominated instrumental music at the English Court for three generations, from 1540 until the death of Charles I in 1649. One hundred years and six monarchs.

1569

Emilia is born and christened Aemilia Bassano on January 27th at St-Botolph-without-Bishopsgate, London.

1576

Death of Baptista, when Emilia is seven years old. She is sent to live with Susan Bertie, Countess of Kent.

1587

Death of Emilia's mother, Margaret Johnson. The Johnsons were also a family of prominent court musicians. Margaret's nephew, Robert Johnson, wrote many of the musical compositions for Shakespeare's plays. There is no record of Emilia's father and mother ever being married.

1587

Emilia catches the eye of Henry Carey, the Lord Chamberlain, and the most powerful man in England (below the Queen). Thirty years his junior, she becomes his mistress and is kept with great pomp and care.

1590–93

Henry Carey becomes the patron to Shakespeare's theatre company and renames it "The Lord Chamberlain's Men."

1592

Emilia becomes pregnant. The Lord Chamberlain marries her off to her first cousin once removed, Alfonso Lanier. The Laniers were also court musicians and both families often intermarried. The marriage was reportedly deeply unhappy and plagued with many miscarriages.

1593
Emilia's son Henry is born.

1598
Emilia's daughter Odillya is born, but dies at 10 months old.

1611
At 42 years old, Emilia publishes *Salve Deus Rex Judaeorum* (Hail God King of the Jews), a proto-feminist volume of poetry. It was likely the first book of original poetry published by a woman in England. She was also the first woman in England to proclaim herself a professional poet and actively seek patronage.

1613
Death of Alfonso Lanier. Emilia begins supporting herself by running a school for young girls, but disputes over rent and questions over her teaching led to her being arrested twice. Parents proved more and more unwilling to send their children to her and the school had to close.

1633
Emilia's son Henry dies, and court documents suggest that Emilia went on to raise and support her two grandchildren.

1645
Emilia dies at 76 and is buried at Clerkenwell.

Some Intriguing Facts:

- The fresco in Bassano del Grappa seems to have truly existed. Greatly faded fragments are preserved in a museum in Bassano. There was both an African and a Jewish community in Italy at the time. Records indicate there were two apothecary shops in Bassano's town square: one run by someone known as "The Moor" and the other part-owned by someone named Giovanni Otello.

- Susan Bertie, the countess that schooled Emilia in her youth, had a younger brother named Peregrine Bertie, Baron Willoughby. Willoughby was sent to Denmark on a diplomatic mission in 1582 and stayed at Elsinore castle. He wrote long letters to his family about his time at Elsinore. 1582 would have coincided with the time Emilia was staying with Susan. *Hamlet* is set at Elsinore castle.

- There is documentary evidence of Wriothesley, the Earl of Southampton, supporting Emilia and her husband financially in 1607. He seems to have known them both.

- In 1584, Emilia's first cousin, Arthur (Arturo) Bassano was arrested for a misdemeanour on Creechurch Lane in London near a secret synagogue. In 1585, Arthur's brother, Mark Anthony Bassano, was arrested for offensive comments to soldiers departing for Flanders. In court depositions, John Spencer, the Sheriff of London, referred to Arthur as "a little black man" and to another Bassano brother as "a tall black man."

- It seems both Quincy Jones and Tennessee (Lanier) Williams are Emilia's distant great-nephews.

Pandora

"It is only in interactions that nature draws the world."
—Carlo Rovelli

Acknowledgements

Rodrigo Beilfuss, Thomas Morgan-Jones, jaymez, Fiona Mongillo, Karyn Kumhyr, Lovissa Wiens, Brenda McLean, Sarah Malabar, Lisa Li, Brian Drader, Jeremy Der, Terry Gallagher, Leif Norman, Lizabeth Kogan, Carman Johnston, Wayne Buss, Deborah Gay-de Vries, Elana Honcharuk, Cherry Karpyshin, Sean Neville, Cari Simpson, Steven Vande Vyvere, Denby Perez, Julia Ross, Haanita Seval, Madeline Sweetland, Haley Vincent, Ntara Curry, Teri-Lynn Kosinski, Fisher Wohlgemut, Tiff Taylor, Kate George, Seraph-Eden Boroditsky, Claire Thérèse Friesen, Christine Kennedy.

I'd also like to acknowledge the following books:

Until the End of Time, The Elegant Universe by Brian Greene, *The Order of Time, Helgoland, Reality Is Not What It Seems* by Carlo Rovelli, *Probable Impossibilities* by Alan Lightman.

Designer's Notes

January 4th, 2022, I received an email from Rodrigo Beilfuss, AD of Shakespeare in the Ruins, asking if I'd be interested in being the production designer for a new play he was directing called *Pandora*. The title grabbed my attention. I had just booked an appointment for a rather large pandemic-inspired Pandora tattoo, so it all felt serendipitous.

The script is all the things I love: mythology, history, quantum physics, real nerd shit. It is such a wonderful text that there was no shortage of inspiration and no hesitation to say yes to the opportunity. It wasn't my first production design, but it would certainly be my most ambitious. Lighting, video, sound and set, all conceived to work together to support this epic script.

I joined Jessica and Rodrigo for an in-depth week-long workshop about a month before rehearsals began. We spent the week brainstorming, reading the play, discussing mythology, quantum physics, Aronofsky, Bergman, art, life, theatre and what all that means after two years of pandemic-driven uncertainty. I left the workshop with more questions than answers, but titanic amounts of inspiration.

A whirlwind of production began as we finalized the set design. Earlier ideas of a flower, an orchid or an iris, were replaced by a 10-foot bronze cube: a cube within a cube, its walls hollow frames, except for the two upstage ones, which served as projection screens. The cube was offset and skewed, jutting from the theatre floor as if it had teleported into place, too big for the black box theatre which it inhabited. At the centre of the cube, sat a smaller white cube: a box with a crank, containing all the mysteries of the universe. This box was projection-mapped and became fire, stars, particles, and a big red button while Jessica conjured big bangs and black holes on the projection screens behind her.

My favourite element of the show was our use of shadows. Live and projected shadows would give Jessica a scene partner, or three. A choreographed duet featured a prerecorded shadow mirroring Pandora's movement, and together they danced across the quantum field; the present and the past in sync with one another.

To create the mythological Underworld, Pandora was lit by a strategically placed footlight as she began her voyage behind the screens. Cast across the white, static flicker of a film projector that's run out of film, her shadow seemed to descend into the stage until she disappeared, leaving nothing but the grainy screens and her voice. Shadows, both real and recorded, took us underground. They became gods. They helped explain why we are and we aren't at the same time.

We travelled with Pandora through time and space, exploring the history of...everything. I'll forever be grateful for the opportunity to collaborate with Jessica and Rodrigo and so very proud of the show we created. A huge thank you to all the staff and crew at SIR and PTE. We couldn't do it without you.

Much love and gratitude, xo

jaymez

September 2023

Production History

The first draft of *Pandora* was originally commissioned by Here for Now theatre for a public reading in Stratford, Ontario, in September 2021. (Its original title was *In Search of Catharsis*.) The cast was Jessica B. Hill.

Pandora was first produced at Prairie Theatre Exchange's Colin Jackson Studio Theatre (PTE) as a co-production between Prairie Theatre Exchange and Shakespeare in the Ruins (SIR). It opened in Winnipeg on January 26, 2023. The play was developed and workshopped with generous support from SIR, PTE and the Manitoba Association of Playwrights. The premiere cast and creative team was as follows:

Pandora ....Jessica B. Hill

Director .... Rodrigo Beilfuss

Production Designer ....jaymez

Production Design Assistant................ Lovissa Wiens

Costume Coordinator ....Brenda McLean

Stage Manager.......................................Karyn Kumhyr

"I went down to the Underworld..." Jessica B. Hill as Pandora. Photography: Joey Senft.

"They discovered a bright face in the sand..." Jessica B. Hill as Pandora. Photography: Joey Senft.

"We are not living in uncertainty. We ARE uncertainty. We're waves of probability." Jessica B. Hill as Pandora. Photography: Joey Senft.

Pandora finally peers into the box. Jessica B. Hill as Pandora. Photography: Joey Senft.

Characters

Pandora: ageless, empathetic, profoundly curious.

Setting

As if in a cave. Or a box. In a box.

The tone should feel unadorned, grounded, intimate.
The scope of the story continually grows and shrinks, from
the unfathomably big to the infinitesimally small.

The original production featured projection screens on the two
walls of the set (a giant cube frame). The projection imagery
heightened the storytelling by adding ambiance, grounding
the space or evoking tiny particles, stars and galaxies. The
screens were sometimes referred to and interacted with.
Walking behind the screens projected shadows of the actor,
either smaller or larger than life. Live and prerecorded shadows
were used to add to the effect. Notes about many of the original
production's special effects can be found in footnotes in the text
of the play.

The frame of the set itself also gave an exciting optical illusion:
the actor appeared taller than the structure when outside the
frame, and smaller once inside.

Stillness.

Dimly lit. As if inside a cave.
Shadows are cast on the walls that seem larger than life.
As the room brightens we see PANDORA, kneeling, cradling a box.

The tone is eerie and grand. A theatrical crescendo of shadows, particles, galaxies, lights or sound. Something majestic as she rises.

Like the birth of a galaxy.[1]

Then.
She smiles at the audience and drops the pretense, instantly shifting the tone.

PANDORA: …
What'd you think?
Too… *theatrical?*

I didn't know how to begin.

Maybe we should just…

Hi.
It's good to see you.

---

[1] *In the original production, Pandora's shadow was cast on both sides of the cube as two prerecorded videos. Pandora rose ritualistically along with her shadows, but suddenly they began to move independently of her. Each shadow struck a match in its own way, lighting a bright flame. The flames danced on the screens, sending tiny particles of light up into the air that swirled and expanded like stars in a galaxy.*

Thank you for being here.
Sharing the space.

This exact combination of people, in this time and place, has never happened before and will never happen again in the history of the universe.

I mean, that's…
Take a moment with that.

> *Beat.*

All good?

(To one specific person.) Do you need more time?
It's okay, we'll wait.

(Checks in with the same person.) You done?
I know… It's a lot to take in.

> *She puts the box down and produces a small hand crank.*

> *She purposely holds it up. Then, cheekily gives it a spin.*[2]

Everything in the universe is either a weasel or not a weasel.

> *She inserts the crank into the box.*
> *She is about to turn the crank, but stops.*

Here we go.
But once we choose to begin…
The only way forward is through.

---

[2] *In the original production, a pedestal was built at the centre of the cube structure. Pandora placed the box on the pedestal and the box reacted to being set in its proper place. Lighting and sound were used to give the box its own vocabulary and agency. Its two visible sides were used as smaller projection surfaces allowing it to transform and interact with the story (It became an ancient box, a primordial fire, a supernova, a red button, etc.)*

Shall we?

She gingerly turns the crank.

The familiar first few notes to "Pop goes the Weasel" play.

Welp. No turning back now.

Now it's just all about *when*.

Pause.

Come to think of it:
Even a weasel isn't a weasel.
It's just a collection of particles that make up
a creature that we've called… "weasel."

…there's no such thing as a weasel.
We labelled a box.
We made it up.

And if even a weasel isn't a weasel…
Then maybe Everything is Nothing.
Or Everything is Everything.

Pause.

I overthink things.

You noticed?

It's also entirely possible that I've gone mad.
Oh well.

Pause.

…I'm meandering
…this is harder than I thought…

I gathered you here… to…
Well…

She sighs.

…I have to apologize.

I'm sorry.

Remember the plague?

Yeah. That one.
It was my fault. Apparently.

But it's not just that…
I have to apologize for… Everything.
All of it.

I am sorry.

I am so, so sorry.

I'm sorry for… traffic. That's me.
The stain on your brand new shirt. Also me.
Droughts.
Tornadoes.
Hurricanes.
That word on the tip of your tongue.
Forest fires.
Floods.
Famines.

Plagues. All of 'em, all the plagues. Sorry.

(Grimaces.) Intermittent wifi.

Ever walk into a room and forget why you came in? *(Points to herself and nods.)*

From stubbed toes to sinkholes…
If something unpredictable happens that messes up your plans,
it's all my fault.

I call them… weasels.
The unexpected wrenches in the machine.

They lie in wait...ready to pop up and remind you what little control you actually have over your life.

I unleashed the weasels on humanity.

Sorry.

For centuries, seeing a weasel in the wild was considered bad luck.
Which is a shame because... they're really cute.

But they're also stealthy, vicious, destructive...
And can pop up at any time.

So yeah... I'm sorry about the weasels of the world.
...

It was an *accident*.
It happened so fast...all I could do was watch.

And I know, you're going to want some answers...

Just know, I've been trying to fix it.
For CENTURIES.
Trying to make sense of it all.
...And I don't know what to do...

All of this because of my stupid curiosity.
All of this because I opened... a stupid box.

> *Pause.*
> *Refers to herself.*

Pandora.

The woman with the box?

I look different than what you imagined?

You were thinking a toga or a loose flowy
sheet?
Yeah.
...we'll get to it.

But, it's me.
Pandora.
The first woman ever, according to the
Greeks.
Intentionally created to doom humankind
to an eternity of unexpected suffering and
frustration.

"Allegedly."

> *Beat.*
> *She looks up in the sky to make sure no one*
> *is listening.*
> *She comes closer. In a conspiratorial tone.*

...Can I set the record straight?

I think I was set up.

I mean...
What if the box was empty?

What if the gods started to notice the world
didn't run as smoothly as they first thought?

What if it was too chaotic,
Too full of random mayhem,
... and they needed a scapegoat.

Why not the first woman ever?
...

> *She chuckles.*

No proof or anything... just a sneaking
suspicion.

...

The gods made me themselves,
Out of dust and water.
I "popped" into existence.

Sounds charming?
It wasn't.
Sudden corporality is deeply uncomfortable.
It's blindingly bright.
It feels like pins and needles.
Picture your leg falling asleep...
Yeah, like that. But everywhere.

POP!

(She squints painfully.) "Where am I?

—Welcome, Pandora!
What a looovely name.
Did you know your name means "all of the gifts"?

—It—it does?

—You're gonna be the bearer of "all of the gifts" to humanity! Yay.

—That sounds intense.

—Nah.
Time to give you some of those gifts!
Here! Have an insatiable curiosity about the world around you.

> *The gift immediately takes effect and PANDORA is amazed by the world around her.*

—Oh! Oh! Oh! Oooh!

—Now here, have a mystery container full of *secrets!*

PANDORA suddenly sees the box and is deeply intrigued.

—Oh...?

She approaches but, before she can touch it.

—Ah-ah-ah. Don't you dare open it.

—What? But...
Why are you giving me this? Shouldn't you keep it?

—No. No no no. We're good. Have fun!"

Assholes.

Spitefully cranks the box, a few more notes play.

Look.
Whether it was my fault or not, I'm sorry.
And trust me, I've paid for it.

They've kept me around all these years, so I could witness the damage I've done.
That's my punishment.
"The first of our kind...Cursed to witness all the days of our kind."

The pain I've caused. The shame. The frustration.

Oh, the humanity.
From beginning to end.

Beat.

Have you ever made a bad decision, and had to live with the consequences?
I'm not talking about getting a bad haircut or the wrong couch, I'm talking *regret.*

That deep gnawing at your stomach and twisting at your heart.
Can't turn back. No do-overs. No remedy.
…

I opened the box.
…

Of course I opened the box.
Wouldn't you?

>   *Beat.*

Actually….
It wasn't even a box.
It was a jar.

Yeah. Did you know that?

>   *She chuckles.*

A clay jar.
Shaped like an upside-down egg.
Top-heavy, tippable.
Beige.
…Apparently the perfect place to seal all the evils of the world.

It was a jar like all my other jars. Nothing special.
It was theirs. I figured they'd come back for it, eventually.
But it just sat there gathering dust. Being all big and beige.
And one day, I got bored and I opened it.
….

No good?
Too… beige?

…A box sounds better, doesn't it?
Opening a box feels more mysterious.

It's a better story.
And I get it, you needed a good story.

…

A small golden box has been sitting in my house for weeks, months. (*Neither of which has even been invented yet.*)
It shimmers in the gentle rays of the sun.
Catching my eye. Over and over.
I can almost hear it calling to me.
I'm enthralled… I'm obsessed.
Nothing in the world matters to me but WHAT is in this box and WHY.

One day, the *need to know* is too much to bear.
I dramatically rise and make my way over, as if hypnotized. I lay a hand on either side.
…and I pop open the lid.

…

She smiles. This story's more recognizable.

Better?

A good story sticks.
It sprouts different versions, they branch out, they superimpose.
It takes on a life of its own.
Witnessed by enough people, stories can exist outside the box that contained them, and travel across space and time.

…

Box, jar, it doesn't matter…
I opened it.

And a voice booms…
It tells me I've cursed humankind.
I've soiled the name of ancestor.
Just like that.
Generations upon generations will "recoil in horror when they hear my name."

A bit much.

But at the time…

…at the time

It feels like the world is ending.
My ears buzz. My cheeks flush.
And I run.
I run and run without looking back.
I run until the sun sets.
Until it's so dark I can't see in front me.
My feet bruised and bleeding from the rocks
and weeds.

When I finally stop, bone tired and terrified….
I see a flickering light in the distance.
A gathering of men…

I see a fire. The Fire.

I had never seen one before.

Crackling, golden flames licking the air.
So bright and powerful and dangerous it
pulls you in.

And as I get closer I recognize the men.
It's Prometheus and some of his friends.
Their glowing faces floating in the dark.
Roasting meat from their hunt.
They're surprised to see me but make room.
Someone tosses me the wineskin.

I didn't know it then, but this was the first
gathering around a campfire…ever.

What is it that happens when people gather?
A softening? A quieting of the heart?

A shared witnessing of the now…?
…

We sit in silence. Presence.
Then out of that silence, one of them starts telling us a story to pass the time.
A story about the world and how it came to be.

"There was nothing but the dark void of Chaos,
Until the bright light of Inevitability pierced through the dark.
And from the union of the two the entire Universe was born,
From the Heavens above our heads to the Underworld beneath our feet."

It was the first story.

He's beautiful as he tells it. Magnetic.

And I'm riveted.
Suspended in a larger now.
Trying to block out what's past and what's to come....
... the curse I've unleashed
...the anger of the gods

...I soiled the name of ancestor, they said.

Then, the man telling the story, the first story, puts his hand on my shoulder and smiles mysteriously, as if reading my mind.
All he says is: "Hope."

But...there's this imperceptible shift.
A heightening. A twinkle in his eye...

I bristle.
He isn't one of us...

Suddenly I see him. Really see him.

Dionysus
in disguise.

The Masked God.
The god of liminal states.
The god of the edges of humankind.

Discovered, he sheds his cloak and grows,
and grows until he towers over me.
He smiles again...mysteriously.
Hauntingly....
I brace myself... for what's coming...

...And he disappears.

"Hope."

Stunned, curious, all I can do is sit in silence
and watch the primordial fire pop.
Random tiny sparks as it eats away at the
logs until there's nothing left but glowing
embers and dust.

You've been fascinated with fire ever since.
With opening boxes of your own too.
I've been watching.

> *Pause.*

That was a long time ago.

> *A shift in demeanour. She rolls up her
> sleeves/ties her hair up.*

I'm a scientist now.
Quantum mechanics.

I know.
Big pivot.

It's been a time.

I smash particles together for a living.

I work at CERN, at the largest and most
powerful man-made machine.

It's called the Large Hadron Collider. Heard of it?
We collide the tiniest of particles at nearly the speed of light.
They explode, and then we observe the results.
Hoping to make sense of the entire universe.

We look to the infinitely small to explain the infinitely large.
It's a spooky field of research.

My entire life, I've been seeking for a way to fix what I've done...
To find you answers. Meaning....

The research we're doing comes close.

But how I got here is a long story...

See, way back in the day,
People didn't know how things worked or what to blame when something went wrong.

Everything was spooky.

And no one really had an answer.
So we just ordained a god to everything instead.

Lightning hits a tree!
Oh no! Is Zeus angry?? ...uh........S-Sacrifice a goat?

A devastating flood!
We must appease Poseidon. Sacrifice the goat.

Our crops won't grow!
We're sorry Demeter! Please accept this goat!

The wind is blowing the wrong way!
Shit.
This one's hard. It's got to be big.
Okay. okay. Hear me out.
What if we sacrificed a virgin at the top of a
cliff—
…Hold on, is that a goat?
Bring it over, two for one.
Gods love goats.

Appease the gods with an offering, and your
day gets better.
If they favour you.

Pretty straightforward.
You might say it was a simpler time.

…Try telling that to the goats.

 Pause.

And yet somehow, at that time, there was
also a lot of great thinking going on.

One guy, this philosopher named
Democritus—carefree, cheery, such a great
laugh—he suggested that everything in the
universe was made of tiny particles and
empty space.
Atoms and void.

Just a thought. 2400 years ago. On a Tuesday.
I was there. I watched him have it.
While sitting at a play, an ancient Greek
philosopher stumbled on a theory of the
universe.

…And everyone hated it. All of it.
No one believed it because no one could see
it.
It was *too* spooky.

His idea got buried. Forgotten.

It took *millennia* for someone to come along and rediscover it.

…Einstein.
It was EINSTEIN!

On a Tuesday. While playing violin. One man unlocks the atom and discovers the General Theory of Relativity.
A theory that explains so much of all THIS.

But as soon as he thought he had "the answer," a huge problem popped up.

His beautiful formula that explained the entire universe, was incompatible with *particles*.…the building blocks that make up the entire universe.

And to this day, we haven't figured out what to do about it.

A whole new field of research was born…
And now we have two theories on how the world works.
General Relativity for the large and Quantum Mechanics for the small.

In the world of Relativity, things are linear, continuous, and deterministic.
There's a cause and an effect.
But the rules fall apart when applied to tiny scale.

In the world of the Quantum, everything is based on probability and uncertainty, there is no definite outcome.
But if you took those rules and went too big, you could create a black hole that swallows up the universe.

Quantum Mechanics defies logic.

It makes you have to think outside the box.[3]
…

Democritus was right: Everything in the Universe is *particles*.
Tiny particles, and empty space.

But… here's the catch:
Particles aren't even particles.
First, they're waves.
Waves of Probability.
Undulating in superposition, in many places at once,
Rippling across a quantum field,
Encompassing everywhere a particle might be.

They only become particles when they're *observed*.
When they're in relationship to something else.

Interaction can also make particles entangle together,
And once they are, they can affect each other, even across *space and time*.

(To two audience members.) Hi. Could you both do me a favour?
Glance at each other. Quickly.

You're entangled particles.
And you *(First person.)* are sitting exactly where you are now while you, *(Second person.)* are somewhere in the distant past…
all the way back in Ancient Greece.
And you both have a sealed box with a glove in it.

---

[3] *In the original production, Pandora cheekily steps outside the frame of the cube, knowingly stepping outside her own box.*

If you open your box and find a left-handed glove, yours would BECOME right-handed. Each glove was existing as both right and left...until one of you opened your box and saw your glove.

Here is the crux: We can't ever catch a glimpse of those gloves existing in both states at once, so it's impossible to see entanglement.

Quantum Reality is a leap of faith:
Nothing can be said to exist until it is observed.
And viewing something changes both what is viewed and the viewer.

> *She furtively glances at the box. Then shakes her head.*

...I really hope there's no cat in there...

...

Have I lost you?

Einstein hated it. All of it.
He called it "Spooky action at a distance."

It was the wrench in his machine.
His own personal, tiny weasel.
It bothered him the rest of his life.
...

And, well... It's been driving me crazy ever since because...
Though we may be a long way from sacrificing goats,
We are living with a pretty massive problem.
We have two valid theories to explain how the world works.

But they are completely incompatible descriptions of Reality.
So which one is Real?

Is everything deterministic, linear and logical?
Or probabilistic, chaotic and unpredictable?

Or have we been looking at it all wrong?

Is there a way to connect the two?

Inevitable unpredictability. Deterministic chaos.

She gets excited.

My work at the lab is aiming to do just that.

Create an even bigger theory to encompass it all.

The Answer.

The God Equation.

The Theory of Everything.
…

We're not even close.

She cranks the box for reassurance, a few more notes play.

"The readiness is all."

(*Referring to the box.*) We all know it's coming…but when.
The Illusion of Control.

It dawns on her.

An operating manual would have been nice.
No?

A book of instructions on Living, with the answer to everything?

But there are so many possible factors.
Things that "could" happen, choices you "could" make...

Besides, you have Google now.

That takes care of most of it.
Not all of it...

...Definitely not all of it.

>*Pause.*

It's easier to write instructions on what *not* to do, instead.
What boxes you shouldn't open.

I've watched you write those.
You've written lists and lists of "Do Not Open"s...

But they don't seem to work either, do they?
Nothing seems to stay buried for long.

...I mean... *I* was given a pretty simple instruction... and...

>*She looks at the box. It's doing something seductive. She shares a look with the audience.*

I got curious. So do you.
It's one of our only constants.
Both a blessing and a curse.

... it's what killed the cat.

No cat was or wasn't harmed in the telling of this story.

>*A shift of tone.*

You know what, let's play "would you open it"!

Let's start with the obvious.
Ancient Egypt. You're exploring the great pyramids when you suddenly discover the tomb of a notorious pharaoh. The door is sealed shut... but you can make out a chiselled inscription on the stone:

"For all men who enter this tomb, there will be judgment. An end shall be made for him. I shall seize his neck like a bird, and place the fear of myself into him."

What do you think? Do you open it?

Or wait, you might know this one:

"Good friend, for Jesus' sake forbear
To dig the dust enclosed here;
Blessed be the man that spares these stones,
And cursed be he that moves my bones."

The rest is silence.

That's William Shakespeare under there.
The Einstein of Theatre.
You'd think people would leave him alone...
He gave pretty clear instructions.

Nope... his skull's missing.

Grave robber? Conspiracy theorist?
Ancient method actor struggling with playing Hamlet?

Someone at some point thought: ...."You know what? I want that head."

...

NOW.

Entertain conjecture of a time deep in the future…ten thousand years from now.
You're roaming the earth, in whatever state it's now in… and you suddenly stumble on this.

> *Ambiguous warning images appear on the walls. They are all "long-term nuclear waste warning messages," pictorial warning attempts for the deep future, but none of them should reveal this fact just yet. They appear one at a time.[4]*

…do you open it?

> *Another image appears.*

How about now? Curious?

> *Another image appears.*

Or now? Mysterious…

> *The final image appears. The text large enough to be read by the audience.*

Or what about this one?
If you're somehow able to decipher English.

"This is not a place of honour. Nothing valued is here. This message is a warning about danger."

These are actual instructions made to warn the deep future.
To attempt to prevent people… or whatever comes after people, from digging up nuclear waste.

---

[4] *In the original production these long-term nuclear waste warning images were projected on the screens of the cube. They should be large enough for the audience to have a reaction to them. The images used can be found at the end of the play. Yes, they are real.*

There's a lot of it underground…like…a lot.
And it will stay lethal for the next 300,000
years.

That might be your greatest box.
Your longest legacy.

And now… the question is, how do you stop
the future from getting curious…? From
wanting to know.

Her attention is brought back to the box.

Because we all just want to know…

Choices. "To crank or not to crank."

She cranks the box, a few more notes play.

Your lives are lived in these tiny choices.
These tiny moments.

Every instant, waves of probability turn
into particles inside you with each decision,
making the probable possible.

And you never know what small choice
could utterly change the course of your
life…

*She addresses a bearded/or long-haired
audience member, in which case it's "cut
your hair."*

Are you debating whether to shave your
beard or not shave your beard?

I like it, by the way, don't do a thing.

But if you were, both futures exist until you
make that choice.
Then if you did decide to shave it, that
reality takes over.

But it's possible the choice "not to shave it"
still exists.
It just splinters off into a parallel universe
that we never get to experience.

Maybe there's something comforting in
imagining that.
A different version of "now."
Because there are so many branching paths
you won't take.

For every choice that you make, there's an
infinite number of choices you don't make.

There are so many more things you'll never
experience than what you will.
Doesn't that thought drive you mad?
Isn't it just impossibly unfair and unsettling?

Yet here you are, making choices daily, on
the fly, every second.
Where to eat lunch? What clothes to buy?
Where to live? What hopes and dreams to
cherish? Or abandon? What colour socks to
wear today?

> *Noticing sock choices on specific audience
> members.*

Interesting choices.

How can you ever be sure each decision was
the right decision?
How are you not weighed down into
paralysis?

Especially knowing it's only a matter of
time before a weasel pops up and ruins
everything.
…

(*To a specific audience member.*) Did you make
your bed this morning?

Sorry.
That's a bit too personal and inconsequential.
Or it's a universal act of cosmic rebellion.
Depending how you look at it.

> *She cranks the box, slowly, a few more
> notes. Her face gets sombre.*

... so...
"Here's the rub"...

If anything can happen,
At any time, for any reason and ruin
everything,
And you have no control of the outcome, no
idea what it would look like or if it will even
be worth doing...
Why would you ever choose to do...
anything?

> *A faint heartbeat can barely be heard that
> slowly grows and grows to fill the room.*

...

...Too dark? That way madness lies?

..."Though this be madness, yet there is
method in it."
....

Dionysus was the god of madness.
...Still is. After all this time.
I've caught glimpses. Never long enough for
him to explain what he meant...

Maybe he *couldn't* leave.
You've made him the god of so many
different corners of humanity...
So many overlapping stories. Entangled
narratives.

Stories that travel across space and time.
That take on a life of their own.

He's the god of theatre, wine, chaos,
madness. Fertile, lush verdant nature...

He's always the god that comes.
The god that comes...
To see what you've done with the place. To
see how it all plays out.

You'd hear his drum. Faintly, at first, in the
distance.
You might mistake it for your own heartbeat.

Here. Now. / Here. Now. / Here. Now. /
Here. Now. / Here. Now.

He's the god that comes.
When we can't see the forest for the trees, or
the trees for the forest.

A gravitational singularity drawing back
together what threatens to fall apart.

A great pull towards the space between
What Is.

> *Her hand pats the beat on her chest. The
> sound grows...*

Do you feel it too?
That pull towards being Everything and
Nothing again?
To be so integral, so interwoven, so beholden
to all things that my atoms are yours and
yours are mine?
...

Remember?
A time before Restless Time?
When all was Still, Whole and Home.

When All That Now Is was contained in that first bright dot of light piercing through the dark.

> *She cups her hand as if to hold that first bright dot of light, extending it out to the audience.*

If we could *remember*.
Catch a glimpse.
Pinpoint that exact moment…
Before choices and curses and burdens…
Before there was even the question WHY.
Then maybe we could answer:

"What is this quintessence of dust?"
…
…

"The first of our kind, cursed to witness all the days of our kind."

I wanted to turn that punishment into an offering.
A gift.
I wanted to be a good ancestor.

…….if I was going to be around forever…
I figured I'd dedicate my life to the search.

First it was oracles, animal entrails, divination.
Then I was a pilgrim, a monk, a whirling dervish.
I tried bloodletting, mountain climbing, tea leaves.
Alcohol, drugs, spinning, chanting, meditation.
I sought out gurus, I tripped on magic mushrooms, I licked way too many jungle toads.

I shaved my head, I floated in the Dead Sea,
I danced in the rain until I thought I'd melt.
I travelled to sacred temples, shrines,
churches, cathedrals, silent retreats, sweat
lodges.
I. have. looked.

But the more I poked at an answer, the more
questions came tumbling out.

I was at a loss.

So I went down to the Underworld.[5]
I found a passage down a deep dark cave.
I crossed the river Styx.
The Ferryman… the fermented smell of the
water.
The shadows of all the people who had
fallen.
My heart in my throat.
…

And… when I got there.[6]
It was empty. Abandoned.
There were no gods left.
…

I was alone.
…

It was empty space.
And restlessness.

…This sinking feeling, this quivering inside.

---

[5] *The original production featured several moments where Pandora disappeared
behind the screens of the cube and continued the story through shadow, the
journey to the Underworld was one of them.*

[6] *The original production chose to represent the nothingness of hell with bright
white light and the skipping of the end of a film reel on the screens. Pandora was
behind the screens, black shadow on white background.*

He wasn't out there watching?
Or maybe he was but he didn't want me to
see:

Because viewing something changes both
what is viewed and the viewer......

> *The light becomes blinding. And softens*
> *into daylight.*
> *From sterile nothingness to abundance of*
> *life.*

Next thing I know I'm back outside.
Squinting in the sun.
It's spring.
The birds are chirping.

Everything is lush. Sprouting. Blooming.
And it's.... It's wonderful.
But... I.... can't....
It's not...

I crumple at the foot of a tree.
My head in my hands.
I'm tired....so tired.... From *the need to know.*
It's rage. No... no, it's fear. ... it's a longing.
A longing so powerful towards... *Belonging.*
I look at the world around me... Nature...
just... living.
Effortlessly.
And then, I realize I'm jealous of birds, of
fish, of trees just for being what they are, so
simply. Intrinsically.

Suddenly...there's a rustling in the nearby
bush, and something dashes out:
A weasel!
He looks as surprised as I am.
We hold each other's gaze, locked in a
primal stillness.
It feels like eternity.
A moment rippling through time.

Me looking down at the weasel and him looking up at me.
His coal black eyes locked into mine.
And…he's tiny.
He's long and thin.
So alert. So beautiful.
What on earth could be "bad luck" about him?

This little creature *is* Nature. Presence.

Humans hang their lives on choices but this weasel lives in necessity.
In what IS, and he throws himself at it with fierceness and grace.

And just when I'm about to break in half,
Just when I decide, you know what, fuck it,
I want to be a weasel too,
This tiny weasel grows and grows and grows…and becomes Dionysus.

The shape shifter. The god that breaks us open.
Dionysus….
Locking eyes with me.
The god that purges the wildness in us all.

He's still smiling mysteriously. Infuriatingly.
I feel the universe inside me caving in… and I just want to scream:
"What?! Hope? IS IT HOPE???!"
But he's gone.

> *A shared moment with the audience. Trying to process it all.*
> *She looks up at the sky…*

"Do you see yonder cloud in the shape of a camel?
Methinks it is like a weasel."

The box begins to play without her having cranked it. She's shocked.
It reaches the end of the "Pop Goes the Weasel" song...but it doesn't open.
She's suspended in anticipation...
And then bursts out a few tentative laughs.

Spooky.

Beat. The box begins to pulse with light and sound. In a low, quiet, different way. It draws Pandora back in. As she attempts to touch the box, the light spills out to fill the space, pulsing on the walls behind her.

A shift in tone, as this spurs Pandora to launch into her next story.[7]

The Large Hadron Collider is a giant underground tube that stretches 27 kilometres across the border from Switzerland, to France, back to Switzerland again. The entire ring is lined with hyper-sensitive magnets to help propel the particles along the tube as fast as possible until they collide.

It is the largest, most powerful machine on the planet.

We're at the cutting edge of making sense of it all.
I'm here because nothing else does.

I'm surrounded by humming computers and shuffling lab coats every day.

---

[7] *In the original production, the box began to pulse, projecting a twisting tunnel of blue light stripes. When Pandora went to touch it, the image transferred from the box to the walls of the set. A giant tunnel of blue pulsing light. It became the backdrop for the Large Hadron Collider.*

But today is special.
After years of meticulous calibration and testing,
After millions of dollars of research,
Today is particle collision day.

Everything has to go right.
The sensors have to capture the moment of impact, in frame, in focus and in time.
It happens in the blink of an eye.
A replication of the Big Bang in tiny scale.

Our head of operations, the top scientist, rises.
Everyone goes quiet and watches him.
This is it. This moment. It's all led to this.
He heads to the front of the room. The main console.

His name is Frank.
I should give you a picture.
He's tall. He has a moustache. Picks his nails when he's nervous.
He likes to slurp his soup.
He's human. Like all of you. He could be any one of you.
But he's got a shininess about him today.
A dedication to the cause.
He's beautiful to witness.

He enters a code and the entire ring of magnets turns on.
A sound of buzzing increases.

Then, he opens a plastic cover, protecting a big red button.[8]
It's not a big red button. I can tell you that right now.

---

[8] *The box turned red, becoming the big red button, in the original production.*

But for the story, let's go with it for dramatic effect.
His hand hovers, he takes a breath…and he goes to press it…..

> Her hand hovers over the "button," she takes a breath and a new idea comes.
> The world shifts.

There was an actor in Ancient Greece, during the Great Dionysia of 408 BC, called Hegelochus.
I knew him. Saw him act.
Great *Agamemnon*.
Decent *Tiresias*.
He was good people. A Great "Tragedian."

The word *tragedy* actually comes from Ancient Greek:
…it means "Song of the Goat."
Yup.
You know it.
They used to sacrifice goats before the show.

But it got a bit too messy. Slippery.
So they started offering live goats to the winners of the play competitions instead.
And as time went on, and goats got pricey, it just became a saying.
The "goat" was the sacrifice of the actors, the play, the story.
An offering to the god to appease the madness in us all.

At this Great Festival, Hegelochus was playing Orestes, a brooding young prince.
His father, the king, has been murdered by his mother and her lover, and Orestes wants to avenge his father's death.
But he spends most of the play in existential crisis rather than acting on it.

Both his mother and her lover are killed.
He gets driven mad.
There's a ghost.
It's pretty much Ancient Hamlet.
Good stories: they tend to stick around.

I'm sitting in the audience. Democritus, that merry philosopher no one believed, he's sitting close by.
There are hundreds of people.
Each negotiating their own idiosyncrasies, choices, regrets and desires.
Profoundly flawed. Dreadfully conscious.
Uncomfortably human.
All focused on a single person on stage.

Hegelochus is tiny from where I'm sitting.
But he's magnetic.
He's giving the gift. Acting his heart out through Orestes' plight.

He's been working on that part for weeks... months.
This play could finally cement him as one of the greats. Transcend him into posterity.

But something's about to happen onstage.
Mid-scene.
An out-of-body experience.
A common one, one that many actors have.

It's when you're in the middle of being witnessed on stage and you accidentally witness yourself.

It usually happens at the precise moment you make the mistake of thinking: "Hey, this is going pretty well..."

Which, unfortunately, is exactly what Hegelochus is thinking as he launches into his rousing monologue.

The line is "After the storm, I see again a calm sea"

But he gets a frog in his throat.
His voice catches, and he messes up the inflection.
It's a slight tonal drop instead of a drop and rise.
But instead of saying "calm sea" in Ancient Greek,
He accidentally says, "After the storm, I see again a *weasel*."

I hear a muffled chuckle.
It echoes across the amphitheatre.
A few titters pop up in the other direction.
Then, Democritus, who'd been trying to hold it in, explodes into a belly laugh and it bursts the dam.
The entire audience erupts in laughter.
It's contagious. And gets louder and louder.
People laugh so hard the play has to stop.
Someone laughs so hard they pee their seat.
It's a fiasco.

An unforgettable moment of group hilarity.
A united sea of laughter.
The story becomes myth, legend.
It takes on a life of its own. It transcends time.
Playwrights make fun of this exact moment for hundreds of years to come.
The only reason we still know Hegelochus's name is because of this one glorious screw-up.

> *She holds a finger up (the one glorious screw-up.) Slowly, she uncurls the rest of her fingers, the open-hand gesture recalling*

Frank about to press the big red button. A look to the audience and suddenly, we're back at the Large Hadron Collider.

Frank is about to press the big red button.
Frank, the man with dedication, who slurps his soup, who wishes he spent more time with his son, who carries deep regret for not realizing the last time he saw his father was actually going to be the last time, is about to press the non-existent giant red button to make particles collide across a 27km tube of magnets at the biggest, most powerful machine made by humankind.

Nothing happens.
He presses again.
Nothing.
Six more times in quick succession.
There's a flicker, a light vrrrrzzzzz, and suddenly POP: blackout.

We all stand there, stunned, in the dark.
The anticlimactic shock is overwhelming.
Every second is costing us millions.

And then, immediately, the wave of blame starts.
There's finger pointing and name calling, frustration, yelling.
We need a scapegoat.
We don't know the cause.

But what we do know is that the short circuit came from somewhere along that 27km tube of magnets.
It's a coin toss to see who's going to walk the entire perimeter...
And it lands on me.

I slip on my trek shoes and ride the elevator up.
157 meters to the surface.
The sun makes me squint… It's spring.

I walk the perimeter of the largest, most powerful machine on earth.
From Switzerland to France and then back to Switzerland again.

I finally reach the power station.
And I find the problem.
The cable is severed in two.
Ripped down to the copper wires.

I grab both ends…
Are those…. *teeth marks* on the rubber?

I search the area…

And…. Fifteen feet away, no doubt flung into the air by the strength of the electric current coursing through its tiny veins…
Are the charred remains of a curious, little weasel.

The weasel that stopped the most powerful machine on earth.

Unbelievable part of the story?
It happened again.
Same story. Same scenario.
Eight months later.

ZZZZ
Power kaput.
What the hell?
Walk walk walk walk walk..
Power station.
Cable.
Bite marks.

POP GOES WEASEL.

Beat.

It happened. Twice.

Google it.

Google Hegelochus too while you're at it.

…

The Large Hadron Collider had to be shut down for three years.
Hegelochus never acted again, his career was ruined.

Weasels.

…

… I never went back.
I hadn't told you that.

I'm not sure why…

Because it was absurd? Because life is?

Because viewing something changes both what is viewed and the viewer.

Because, for all I know, my particles and the weasels' were entangled and used to live side by side on the surface of a dying star.

Because……it suddenly wasn't enough anymore.

…

She comes closer.

It's all in how you see it.

Even if we did discover the Theory of Everything…

…It wouldn't *be* everything, would it?

The WHY would still…

The Why…

It's the Why.

…

> *She takes in the audience.*
> *Earnestly, but unsentimentally. To specific*
> *people.*

Alright.
Here it goes.

I'm sorry if things seem to be getting worse
not better.
If you feel like the weasels have gotten
bigger than you.

If you lie awake at night worrying about the
state of the world.
About whether your children or your
children's children will even have a
recognizable future.

I'm sorry for where it all seems to be
heading…
For the greed, the war, the strife.
For rising oceans, and melting ice caps.
For fossil fuels and endangered species.
For all that nuclear waste sealed
underground.

I'm sorry for plastic.
I'm sorry you're now part plastic.

I'm sorry for so many choices your
predecessors made.
Again and again and again.

If you feel betrayed.
If you don't know how to belong.
If you feel like you're going mad because the world isn't quick enough to act, yet everyone thinks that their actions won't *matter*.

I see you. I'm here for you.

But I don't want to be blamed anymore.

Somewhere along the line, it stopped being my fault.
And somewhere down the road...you're going to run out of goats.

I want *you* to be good ancestors.

I know, it's chaos.
I know it's uncertainty.

But we're not living in uncertainty,
We ARE uncertainty.
We're waves of probability.

There's what IS and what CAN BE inside you at all times.
...

...What if this *longing* we feel is just those waves collapsing into particles inside us?
The restless sensation of millions of possibilities hitting dead ends every second of every day?

What if that feeling is the cost of *meaning*?

Because it *could* have gone differently.
Because it *can* still go differently.

What if being curious.... is enough?

...just to make that choice "to begin."

...

She's at a loss.

I didn't know how to wrap things up either.

It's hard to end something when the story's still being written.
...

I wish I could hug each one of you.

You're beautiful.
I needed to tell you that....

And you're more beautiful than when we started.
Somehow. Just from... getting to know you.

A shift. A heightening.
Something in the eyes maybe...

A fire starts crackling. Faint flickering warmth.

I guess I can tell you one last story.
To wrap it up? To... connect the dots?
You can google this one too,
If you need to make it "real."
...

It happened during a plague.

Yeah. That one. Remember?
Stories tend to emerge that way.
Filling the empty space.

But this plague was different from the hundreds I've seen before.

...it was the scale of it.
It hit *all* of humanity.
All at once.

That's never happened before.

And part of it meant that theatres across the entire world shut down.
All at once.

What happens when the whole world can't gather?
Can't share witness? Can't quiet the....
…

Archeologists were digging up the remains of an Ancient Greek city.
At the peak of the plague.
When they hit on something deep in the ground…
They carefully dug and dug….
And piercing through the dark…they discovered a bright face in the sand.
Huge. Bearded. Smiling mysteriously.
A mask of Dionysus.

He'd been dormant, hidden.
Smiling up at us from down there… for millennia.
Just waiting… to be discovered.

The god that cannot be buried.
The god of presence.

She cups her hand and extends it out.

…Remember.

Pause.

Maybe that's it.
All there is.
Cries in the void that it happened and that some of it was awful but a lot of it was beautiful…

And worth retelling, because we saw it happen.
Because it could not have happened, at all.
Random chaos entangling us together...
until, inevitably, there's a story.

Try to write a good one for the people to come.
They're going to want some answers.
...

Hey, don't look at me, you made me up.
What do I know?

Only that the smallest of actions can have the greatest of impacts.

Only that the choices you make become the stories *they'll* tell.

Only that everything can happen, *has* happened and *is* happening.
At the same time, everywhere...including right here. Now.
Infinite *possibility*. In a *tiny*, limited space.
...

> *We start to hear the heartbeat in the distance. It builds steadily..... She taps her chest. The god is coming.*

...I didn't bring a goat.

> *She closes her eyes, and outstretches her arms, offering herself as sacrifice.*

To the God of Gathering!

> *The box pops open and scares her.*

AHHH!!

A bright beam of light shines out of the box.
A message from the gods.

She slowly rises and makes her way over, as
if hypnotized.
She peers inside…..

It's the answer. To everything.
It's beautiful, it's wonderful, it's…
hilarious.
She bursts out laughing.

Mid-laughter, she turns to the audience to
share. It's deliciously simple.

It's—

POP, the lights go out.

The end.

Long-Term Nuclear Waste Warning Images

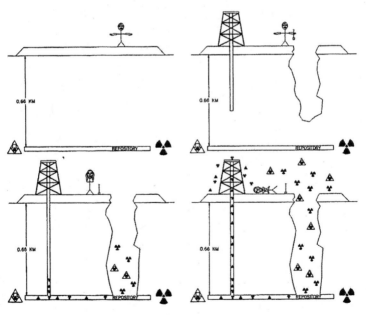

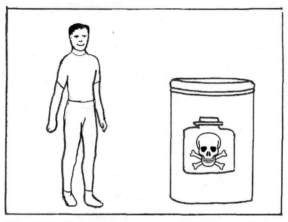

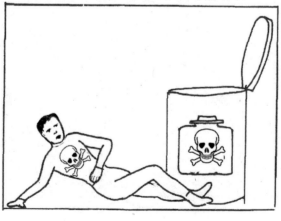

this is not

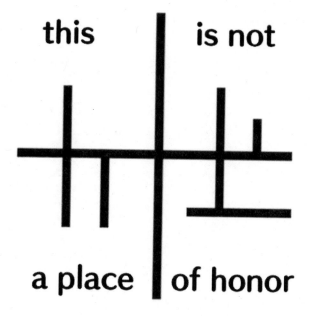

a place of honor